ARCHITECTURE TRANSFORMED

NEW LIFE FOR OLD BUILDINGS

NORA RICHTER GREER

FOREWORD BY
HUGH HARDY, FAIA

First published in the United States of America by
Rockport Publishers, Inc.
33 Commercial Street
Gloucester, Massachusetts 01930-5089
Telephone: (978) 282-9590
Facsimile: (978) 283-2742

Distributed to the book trade and art trade in the United States by
North Light Books, an imprint of
F & W Publications
1507 Dana Avenue
Cincinnati, Ohio 45207
Telephone: (800) 289-0963

Other Distribution by
Rockport Publishers, Inc.
Gloucester, Massachusetts 01930-5089

ISBN 1-56496-456-6

10 9 8 7 6 5 4 3 2 1

Design: Sawyer Design Associates, Inc.
Diane Sawyer, Nina Souther, Amy Weiss

Front cover image: Los Angeles Central Library,
photo by Tim Street Porter

Back cover images: (top) Fleet Bank, before renovation, photo courtesy of
Einhorn Yaffee Prescott; (bottom) Fleet Bank, after renovation, photo by
Bill Murphy.

Front flap image: David Saul Smith Union, Bowdoin College, photo by
Brian Vanden Brink

Interior page images: (page 6) Como Park Conservatory, photo by Brian
Droege Photography; (page 7, clockwise from top left) Shakespeare's
Globe Theatre, photo courtesy of Pentagram Design, Inc.; David Saul
Smith Union, photo © Brian Vanden Brink; Gary Group, photo by Tom
Bonner; U.S. Court of Appeals, photo by Abby Sadin Photography; Furness
Library, photo by Matt Wargo; (page 8, top left) Lingotto Factory, photo
© Gianni Berengo Gardin; (page 8, bottom right) Old Executive Office
Building, photo by Walter Smalling Jr.; (page 9, clockwise from top left)
Shakespeare's Globe Theatre, photo courtesy of Pentagram Design, Inc.;
Lingotto Factory, photo © Gianni Berengo Gardin; Marsh and McLennan
Building, photo by Scott McDonald © Hedrich Belssing.

Manufactured in China.

ACKNOWLEDGMENTS

It has been a great pleasure to gather together such a variety of exemplary preservation projects in Architecture Transformed. *As the author of this book, I would first like to acknowledge the hard work of the architects whose projects appear here.*

Hugh Hardy lent a philosophical tone—and a legitimacy—to the book through his much appreciated foreword. I thank him.

The staff of Rockport Publishers offered support and guidance, and I would particularly like to acknowledge Rosalie Grattaroti for giving me the chance to write this, Martha Wetherill for her unwavering patience, Diane Sawyer for her graphic design expertise, and Madeline Gutin Perri for making sure my words made sense.

Completing this project also required the patience and support of friends and family. I especially thank my husband, William, for cheerfully surviving when deadlines preceded everything else.

CONTENTS

FOREWORD

HUGH HARDY, FAIA

Architectural preservation is a double-edged sword. It enriches our cultural heritage, but if pursued in a doctrinaire way, it stifles new ideas. Although no age has built more rapaciously or at a larger scale than our own, no era has been more earnestly engaged in the attempt to prevent change. But it is no more possible to achieve total architectural preservation than it is to stop physical and social change. Nature opposes both. Taken to extremes, preservation tries to either freeze the status quo through conservation or turn the clock back through restoration. But good architecture defies these purist objectives. Neither pure conservation nor total restoration recognizes the realities of contemporary building codes, lighting levels, environmental systems, security concerns, or the needs of present-day activities.

Older edifices offer insight into the values of their owners, providing historical continuity, whereas many new buildings are found to have no commitment, no sense of place. As the scale, cost, and complexity of new structures increase, the opportunity to imbue them with personal or intimate appeal diminishes. The pervasive blandness of contemporary development, however, has led to the preservation movement, a phenomenon that has had a strong effect on many aspects of contemporary architectural practice.

When the Modernists banished history from architecture in quest of "pure" form, rejecting a built language that linked generations, they created a dilemma for contemporary architects. Even America, conceived afresh in the New World, borrowed heavily from Europe as it cleared land to build new communities. Most of the extraordinary expansion during the nineteenth century was clothed in historical styles, often in a wildly eclectic manner, to create an architecture the scale and complexity of which the world had never seen before. Cornices, columns, arches, traceries, keystones, quoins, and balusters—time-honored ornamental devices—were pressed into high-rise service, lending an accepted civility to a startling new urban landscape.

But when these age-old devices were abandoned by modernists in favor of more abstract ideas about form and function, the field of architecture was split into different camps, some looking to design with traditional massing and ornamentation, and others to creating stark buildings, a breach that is only now being bridged. While architects wrestle with this dilemma, preservation has been embraced by the public as a way to insist buildings offer a sense of connection to our common cultural legacy. Even though preservation can impede new construction, often forcing compromise, the results of these confrontations many times benefit everyone, joining even large-scale development to an appropriate social and historical context.

There is no formula for correct preservation design. What distinguishes the following selection is its variety, a dazzling array of re-use. These examples interpret the past, evoking

the spirit of old buildings while accepting new activities. Some keep to their original purpose. Others encourage radically new activities, but all are united by the belief that structures from another age can be eloquent vehicles for the shelter and expression of contemporary life.

It is through this resolution of conflict between current architectural ideas and those of an earlier era that adaptations of older structures show their true worth. We have every reason to be proud of the age we live in, but it can best be comprehended when compared with those that have come before. Preservation encourages this measurement, enriching our understanding of ourselves even as it reveals the ambitions of others.

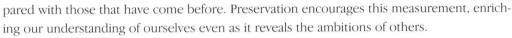

INTRODUCTION

Over the centuries, structures have been built, used, rebuilt, preserved, left to ruin, or torn down. During the twentieth century, however, this natural cycle of habitation accelerated to an extraordinary pace. In our throwaway society, large portions of cities seemed to change virtually overnight to make room for modernization. In response worldwide, but particularly in the West, advocacy for more deliberately planned change grew into a well organized, effective presence, so much so that preservation of our built heritage is now a universally embraced ideal as we strive to perpetuate a sense of place, tradition, and culture. The preservation movement was also fueled by a heightened global

environmental consciousness. We now ponder the resources embodied in an old building as a positive contribution and worthy of conservation. Yet the battle between old and new is never static. Change is inevitable and encouraged, but also welcome are the measures that prevent the demolition of significant buildings and places without public debate.

Architecture Transformed offers a glimpse at the diverse way in which new life has been given to old buildings during the 1990s. The thirty-seven projects seen on these pages are the tip of the iceberg—thousands of buildings have been successfully preserved in this period. These buildings were chosen for their exemplary design sensitivity and to illustrate the astonishing range of preservation architecture. The projects are separated into three sections: restoration and reconstruction, rehabilitation, and adaptive use. It is clear, however, that precise definition can be elusive and that some projects could be classified in several categories at once.

Nothing marks time more precisely than the restoration of a historic building. While it is easier than ever before to determine a building's original appearance—with the help of high technology and preservation experts—it is virtually impossible to undertake a totally pure restoration. This goal seems limited to the historic house museum, like Thomas Jefferson's Monticello, which down to practically every detail appears as it did in the late 1700s. The more realistic challenge in restoration is to so seamlessly introduce contemporary

amenities or to bring a building up to modern code compliance so inconspicuously as not to disturb the original design.

Notice, for example, that there is no sign of what must be extensive state-of-the-art communications equipment in the Secretary of the Navy's Office, now occupied by the vice president of the United States, in the Old Executive Office Building. The New Amsterdam Theater, and other projects, raise the question: Which era of a building's life should the restoration or renovation reflect?

Partial reconstruction is often undertaken if a monumental building is significantly damaged by fire, as at Case Western's Adelbert Hall, or by an earthquake, hurricane, or other natural disaster. The 1989 Loma Prieta earthquake in California spurred extensive seismic upgrading of buildings there, including the U.S. Court of Appeals. Or, part of a landmark structure may desperately need shoring up, such as the skylight system in the great hall of Frank Lloyd Wright's Wingspread, a process that may demand the use of highly innovative modern techniques. It's rare, and therefore quite special, when an entire building is reconstructed, as Shakespeare's Globe Theatre was. The extensive undertaking brought back sixteenth-century construction techniques, some of which may have application today.

While more interpretive than restoration, the rehabilitation of historic structures is a much more extensively practiced preservation method. Taken together, rehabbed buildings make up the fabric of our cities and our collective memories. Often, rehabilitation rather than restoration is the only economic alternative. For example, Fleet Bank was interested in housing its offices in the once grand Union Station in Albany, New York, yet found the move economically feasible only if the usable work space were doubled.

What makes a rehabilitation exemplary is finding that balance between preserving the character of the original building and designing transformations within the building or in the form of additions. The success of the Marsh and McLennan Building, for example, was due to the architect's ability to create a unified statement between a 1904 cast-iron warehouse and a much larger contemporary addition through the use of sympathetic massing and materials. In an unusual turn of events, the exterior of a residential complex at Middlebury College was radically changed from a modern appearance to match the more traditional collegiate architecture found elsewhere on campus.

The practice of adaptive use often brings the most wonderment. A huge waterfront factory is turned into luxury apartments; an old hospital into affordable housing; a college field house into a student center. Architects can take great liberty in adaptive-use designs while perpetuating a sense of place.

RESTORATION, RECONSTRUCTION

RESTORATION

"The act or process of accurately recovering the form and details of a property and its setting as it appeared at a particular period of time by means of the removal of later work or by the replacement of missing earlier works."

U.S. SECRETARY OF
INTERIOR'S STANDARDS

RECONSTRUCTION

"The act or process of reproducing by new construction the exact form and detail of a vanished building, structure, or object, or a part thereof, as it appeared at a specific period of time."

U.S. SECRETARY OF
INTERIOR'S STANDARDS

NEW AMSTERDAM THEATER

NEW YORK, NEW YORK

The return of the once dying New Amsterdam Theater marked a significant recommitment by business and government to New York City's Times Square district. It also advanced the debate over how faithful a restoration should be. Should a building be returned to its exact original appearance, if possible, or should it exhibit the aging that has occurred? What if some additions bring more splendor to the original? For this Art Nouveau theater, an elaborate building that has been called an enchanted forest, Hardy Holzman Pfeiffer Associates chose an interpretive restoration.

The theater had changed dramatically over time. Designed by Henry B. Herts and Hugh Tallant, the 1,750-seat theater opened on October 26, 1903, and was soon hailed as the most gorgeous playhouse in New York. Structurally innovative, it took advantage of skeleton-steel construction instead of the typical masonry, which increased the amount of interior space. It also featured an early cantilevered balcony. The New Amsterdam thrived as the theater of the Ziegfeld Follies until 1927, but in 1937 it was sold and converted into a movie house. Subsequent changes included tearing down the twelve side-boxes to make way for a wide Cinerama screen. The worst deterioration came after the building closed in 1982; the leaking roof ruined the floors and walls, the stairs crumbled, and the elaborate plasterwork turned to rubble. As life-support, New York State bought the theater in 1992 and stabilized the structure. The theater's rebirth wasn't assured, however, until The Walt Disney Company entered into a lease with the city and state to restore and operate the building for its Broadway musical spectaculars.

The extravagance of the interior decorations—from the elaborate peacock proscenium arch to the nymphet heads illuminating columns with halos of incandescent lights—elicits a chorus of superlatives. Extensive research, documentation, and scientific analysis revealed enough of the elaborate details to allow reconstruction of those lost. Through the interpretive restoration, the architect chose to present the passage of time.

Torn down in 1953, the twelve side-boxes were re-created from old photographs. The design of each represents a different flower. The 1937 Art Deco marquee was retained, as it had become a familiar Forty-second Street landmark.

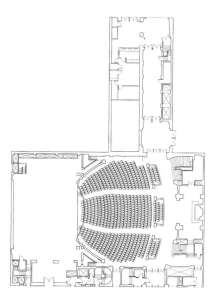

The auditorium's theater is a mind-boggling, splendid extravaganza. Half of the elaborate details were re-created in the restoration. The theater is entered on Forty-second Street through a narrow yet grand promenade decorated with panels that depict scenes from Shakespeare and Wagner.

Originally the Lounging Room, the elliptical New Amsterdam Room on the basement level is ringed with rotund plaster columns resembling gray Caen stone and again with murals of New York City. To produce the same intense color that the theater's guests saw in 1903, colors in the Progress mural were adjusted a few shades so that the theater looked the same under the new house lights as it did in its heyday. The skylight that had been painted over was given new life.

16

The stairs' balustrades are a burnished, dark green terra-cotta with Shakespearean heads.

A crawl space above the stage housed the only original light fixture, a dream maiden adorned with sunflowers and small lights.

The General Reception Room features a vaulted ceiling and dominant fireplace.

FURNESS LIBRARY

UNIVERSITY OF PENNSYLVANIA, PHILADELPHIA, PENNSYLVANIA

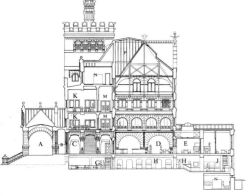

Like any other art form, architectural aesthetics evolve slowly over time, with one generation of architects influencing the next, and on and on. Yet, as time passes, landmark designs are often lost in the name of progress, along with the unique signature of a particular groundbreaking architect. It is not surprising, then, that great excitement and, ultimately praise, surrounds the preservation of an important piece of history. A marvelous example is the University of Pennsylvania library designed by Frank Furness, built in 1888 through 1891, and renovated by Venturi, Scott Brown and Associates, with restoration and historical consultants The Clio Group, Inc., and Marianna Thomas Architects.

Known also for his designs of the Pennsylvania Academy of Fine Arts and the Provident Life and Trust Company building (now demolished), Furness brought to the late nineteenth century a unique vision. His architecture was greatly influenced by structural expressionism, the neo-grec philosophy of Viollet-le-Duc; a Ruskin-like, powerful vision of the role of architectural ornament, and a love of the complex contrasts of color and texture of High Victorian Gothic. Furness was adept at designing buildings whose functions resulted in irregular, asymmetrical exteriors.

By the early 1980s, the Furness Library faced either major restoration or demolition, as neglect and haphazard alteration had transformed it into a white elephant on the University of Pennsylvania campus, where it held a prominent position on the central quadrangle. Restoration presented a complex series of challenges including the insertion of modern structural and mechanical systems as well as bringing the entire building up to current environmental and technological systems requirements.

A phased construction plan began with exterior restoration. The second phase encompassed the renovation of the book-stack building. Restoring the monumental interior spaces made up the third stage. Generations of paint were cleaned from the buff-colored terra-cotta and red brick walls and surfaces were repaired, including the re-creation of carved terra-cotta foliated bands and window surrounds using gypsum-reinforced fiberglass. Ornamental iron-, steel-, and copperwork was restored throughout the building. Lighting fixtures and furnishings, designed to recall lost Furness pieces, were installed in time for the building's centennial celebration in 1991.

A predilection for expressionism marks the architecture of Frank Furness, as seen in the bold forms of the Furness Library at the University of Pennsylvania.

ALL PHOTOS: MATT WARGO

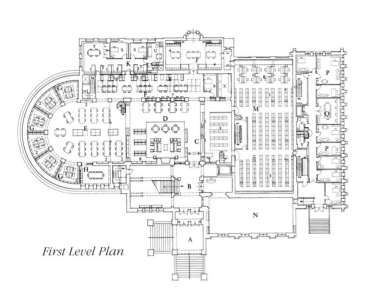

First Level Plan

A meticulous restoration effort brought back the original brilliance of the monumental interior spaces, such as the main reading room.

*The Apse Fine Arts Studio
sits above the reading
room, both of which receive
abundant natural lighting.
Lighting fixtures and
furnishings were redesigned
by VSBA to recall lost
Furness pieces.*

OLD EXECUTIVE OFFICE BUILDING

WASHINGTON, D.C.

The massive, eclectic Old Executive Office Building stands proudly amid extensive site refurbishing. Its showcase is the Secretary of the Navy's office, now the office of the vice president, a room beautifully embellished with gilded surfaces and a wood floor (above).

Pure restoration—that is, returning a building to its exact original splendor—is most often not a possibility. Usually, not only has the use of that building or space changed greatly over the years, but it is also impossible to adequately assess its original appearance. When it does happen, it takes an abundant amount of skill and determination, as with the restoration by Einhorn Yaffee Prescott of the Secretary of the Navy's Office in the Old Executive Office Building (OEOB).

Now the showcase of the OEOB, that room's original ornate decorative surface had been horribly obscured. In fact, many thought the 1879 William J. McPherson original design unrecoverable—rightly so, as restorers found thirteen layers of paint over the original painted and gilded surfaces. Further, the room had been partitioned, obscuring its original dimensions. Using historic photographs as a guide, the room was brought back to its original appearance. The decorative wall design was discovered by carefully erasing the layers on one portion of the room and then using the area thus revealed as a model for the rest. To renovate the floor, a grand search was undertaken for wood to match the color and texture of the original marquetry. Crucial to the success of the project were the seamless concealment of the advanced security and communications system in the floor and the upgraded mechanical and electrical services elsewhere. This room is now used by the vice president of the United States for his office.

It should be noted that Einhorn Yaffee Prescott also renovated other OEOB interior spaces, such as an elaborately detailed skylight deep in the heart of the building. In addition, extensive site work significantly spruced up the exterior of this highly articulated and ornamented Second French Empire building, designed by Alfred B. Mullet and built between 1871 and 1888, which sits directly west of the White House.

*The original surfaces of the
secretary's office had been
obliterated over the years.
A painstaking restoration
brought the splendor back.*

COMO PARK CONSERVATORY

SAINT PAUL, MINNESOTA

onstructed in 1914, Como Park Conservatory is one of the few remaining Victorian greenhouses in the United States. Known as the Jewel in the Crown, it had grown tarnished, its plumbing rusting, the foundation cracked, the electrical systems failing, and the fiberglass wall and ceiling panels yellowed. A high degree of public support, as well as significant financial aid from the state and private organizations, led to the restoration of the conservatory by Symmes Maini & McKee Associates/Winsor Faricy. It was no easy task, given the severe deterioration and the need to keep the conservatory's growing environment stable, a task complicated by Minnesota's harsh climate.

Como Park Conservatory was the lifelong dream of Saint Paul Park Superintendent Frederick Nussbaumer. Born in Germany, Nussbaumer brought to America a vision of the great parks of Europe. He was especially fond of London's Crystal Palace, a giant conservatory built in 1850 with a cast-iron frame and ridge-and-furrow glazing system, a beautiful structure that at its time was at the cutting edge of new technology. It took Nussbaumer twenty years to persuade Saint Paul to build its own Crystal Palace at the heart of a 450-acre (180-hectare) city park. Since its completion in 1914, millions have visited the conservatory—its 64 1/2-foot (19.7-meter) Palm House flanked by two 26-foot-wide (7.9-meter-wide) and 100-foot-long (30.5-meter-long) wings—the Sunken Garden, and the North Wing.

The extensive restoration was accomplished over nine years, as funding was made available. Most visible to the public is the sparkling clear glass that replaced the opaque covering over the central Palm House and the North and South wings. Less obvious, but extremely important, were the repair, replacement, and refinishing of the structural steel frame, replacement of the mechanical and electrical systems, and the installation of customized ventilation systems. The flagstone circulation path was restructured to meet accessibility standards, and the growing houses and hothouses were replaced with a 30,000-square-foot (2,700-square-meter) facility.

Elegantly restored, a classically inspired pavilion welcomes visitors to the Como Park Conservatory. The pathway surrounding Harriet Frishmuth's Crest of the Wave *sculpture in the Palm Dome was reconstructed to meet handicap accessibility standards.*

To reduce solar gain in the summer and to eliminate the need for shading, the glass in the south-facing Sunken Garden is darker at the ridge. Exterior views reveal the conservatory's shape—a central dome flanked by two wings. New growing houses and hot-houses flank the North Wing (opposite, top right).

STANFORD MEMORIAL CHURCH

STANFORD UNIVERSITY, PALO ALTO, CALIFORNIA

The interior of Stanford University's Memorial Church was restored to its original grandeur. The addition of recessed lighting brings more illumination to the strong lines of the wooden ceiling. The building was damaged in the 1906 and 1989 earthquakes (above).

At Stanford University's Memorial Church, Hardy Holzman Pfeiffer Associates achieved the ultimate restoration goal: to so closely restore the building to its original splendor that "it looks like we didn't do anything," in the words of Norman Pfeiffer. Yet, in addition to the restoration work, the firm supervised massive reconstruction to bring the building up to current seismic standards. Precast, steel-reinforced columns hold up new concrete floors, with paint and stucco hiding the reinforcements. In fact, some 470 tons of concrete were poured into the narrow void within the hollow walls. New electric wires snake unseen through the walls as well. While some of the changes are more visible—shotcrete replaces some of the original plaster and the light fixtures are replicas—the clarity and grandeur of the original design has been beautifully revitalized.

The 1989 Loma Prieta earthquake was not the first to damage the church, designed in 1899 by Shepley, Rutan & Coolidge. The 1906 earthquake toppled the church's massive central tower, whose octagonal spire soared to an ornamental cross some 150 feet (45 meters) above ground. When reconstructed, only the substructure of the tower was retained. The Loma Prieta earthquake did, however, send the 8-foot (2.4-meter) mosaic of the wing of the Archangel Uriel crashing some 70 feet (21.3 meter) to the floor of the transept.

The focal point of Stanford University's main quadrangle, Memorial Church was built as a memorial to Senator Leland Stanford by Mrs. Stanford, who, with Leland, founded the university. The church's design, and much of the original campus as well, reflects Charles Coolidge's apprenticeship with H. H. Richardson—carved natural stone, massive columns, low rounded archways, and red tiled roofs set in a cruciform plan. The church is filled with Italian mosaics, all carefully preserved in the restoration. The walls of the nave are embellished by a series of murals, fifteen on each side, depicting scenes from the Old Testament. The central domed ceiling is supported by four pilasters, each with an archangel rising from clouds. Even the exterior has mosaics—the north façade of the church depicts Christ welcoming the righteous into the Kingdom of God.

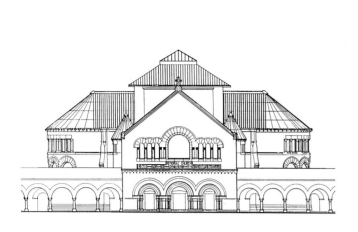

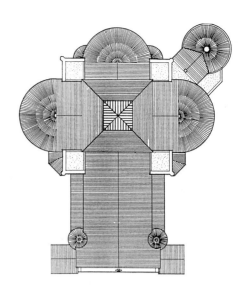

Four eight-foot-tall archangels decorate the upper walls of the transept; one crashed to the floor during the 1989 earthquake.

The door in the upper portion of the west transept was installed after that earthquake. The door itself is new; the brass hinges and glass mosaics around it are original.

JOSEPH PENNOCK HOUSE

CHESTER COUNTY, PENNSYLVANIA

The Joseph Pennock House offers valuable insight into the evolution of architectural styles in Chester County and the nearby Pennsylvania countryside. Abandoned for nearly thirty years, the house now stands as the centerpiece of the Pennock Farmstead, which also contains ten other historic eighteenth- and nineteenth-century buildings. It was built as a three-room house plus adjoining kitchen in 1760 and expanded to a four-bay Georgian plan over the years 1800 to 1812. That design was frozen over time, as no major renovations were undertaken. This allowed Susan Maxman Architects to preserve the integrity of the building in its Georgian plan while carefully inserting modern amenities. The footprints of the three-room house are still visible.

Renovation of the Pennock House was organized into four phases. First came extensive historical research, documentation, and assessment of exiting conditions. The second phase involved structural and exterior surface stabilization and rehab, all undertaken with care not to disturb the house's historic fabric. For example, investigation revealed that the stairwell wall needed underpinning; it was rebuilt with the facing stones replaced in their previous positions. New steel columns and beams were required to support the first-floor joists. The exterior brickwork was in good condition, although advanced weathering of the stone masonry walls required total repointing.

Structural repair and surface fabric conservation was the third step, a task eased because the integrity of the interior finishes remained largely intact. All wood molding and doors were conserved and repairs and replacements made of carefully duplicated materials. The mantles of the five fireplaces were restored with the exception of the kitchen/cooking hearth, which was replicated on the basis of comparable buildings of the same region and period. In the fourth phase, new heating, plumbing, and electrical systems were seamlessly inserted.

Even though extensive restoration was required, before photographs reveal that much of the abandoned building's defining characteristics remained intact. In the renovation, an exiting porch was removed and reinstalled and a new one added in the rear.

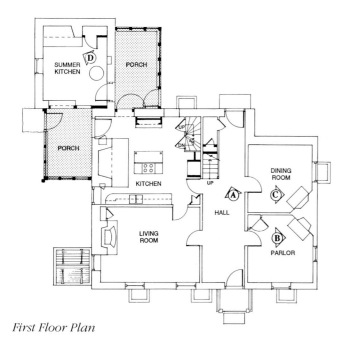

First Floor Plan

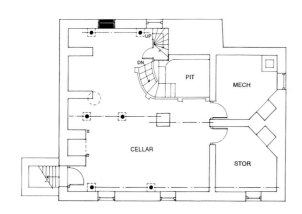

Basement Plan

Floor plans suggest a simple but elegant room arrangement typical of the Georgian style. Interior surfaces were restored or re-created to match the original appearance.

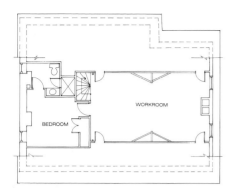

Third Floor Plan

Second Floor Plan

SHAKESPEARE'S GLOBE THEATRE

LONDON, ENGLAND

The meticulous reconstruction of Shakespeare's Globe Theatre was an archeological endeavor involving extensive architectural research as well as revival of sixteenth-century building technologies. The long and spirited campaign to recreate the theater was led by American actor Sam Wanamaker and British architect Theo Crosby of Pentagram, Ltd.; a host of others participated. Historical authenticity was the guiding rule, yet compromises were made to reconcile construction with current building codes and standards. Not only did the effort result in the revival of this famous playhouse but it also demonstrated that traditional materials and construction methods have a role to play in contemporary building.

The first task was to decipher the Globe's original appearance, both exterior and interior. Built in 1599 on the south bank of the Thames River for William Shakespeare's company of players, the Globe achieved quick popularity. In 1613 a spark from a stage cannon set fire to the thatched roof of the theater and it burned to the ground. A second, more ornate theater was built on the same foundations, but it closed in 1644. Extensive research suggested that the theater's shape was a faceted circle of twenty sides or bays. More specifically, the geometry of the theater radiated from a central point, and the form and number of bays were determined by radiating lines set eighteen degrees apart.

To determine the nature and methods of construction techniques used for the Globe, the architect compared buildings of the same form or function and built at the same time in the same geographical area. The conclusion: The Globe was an open-air theater framed in green oak jointed by scribes, with a thatched roof and three-level wooden amphitheater seating. The structure sat on a plinth constructed of Tudor-styled brick and lime mortar. Use of sixteenth-century building materials and techniques revealed how versatile green oak is as a building material.

Research revealed no record of the interior's appearance. Based on information found in books authored by sixteenth-century architects Sebastiano Serlio and Andrea Palladio and in other sources, Crosby concluded that the interior of the Globe would have had a classical veneer and been brilliantly painted.

COURTESY OF THE BRITISH MUSEUM

The centerpiece of a new multiuse complex, the reconstructed Globe Theatre sits in close proximity to its original site on London's Thames River. To rediscover the Globe's original appearance, an in-depth archeological search unearthed numerous representations in drawings.

ALL PHOTOS: COURTESY OF PENTAGRAM DESIGN, INC.

For the theater's frame, sixteenth-century means of scribing oak timbers were rediscovered. Believed to be the first thatched roof applied on a building in London since the great fire of 1666, a layer of fireboard and a sprinkling system were placed underneath the thatch to meet code requirements. Views of the open-air Globe from different angles reveal its unique structure.

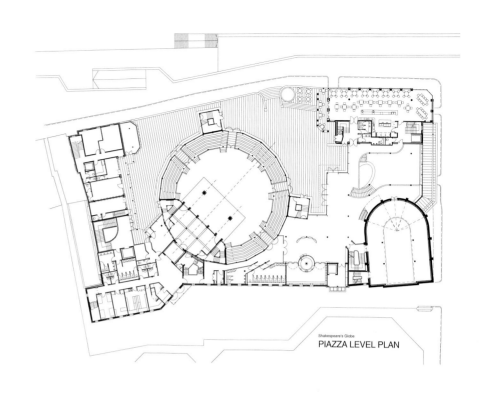

Shakespeare's Globe
PIAZZA LEVEL PLAN

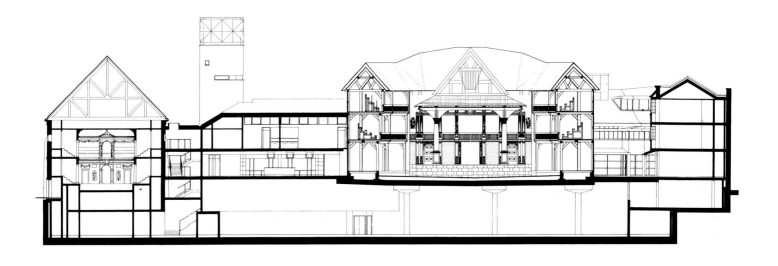

Inside, the Globe Theatre explodes with colorful decoration. The stage becomes a temple portico with Herculean columns supporting gabled proscenium. The canopy above the stage—the area of the theater representing heaven—is adorned with a sixteenth-century rendition of the twelve astrological figures surrounding a supernatural light.

ADELBERT HALL

CASE WESTERN RESERVE UNIVERSITY, CLEVELAND, OHIO

When a devastating fire swept through Adelbert Hall in June 1991, Case Western Reserve faced the loss of more than just the venerable 1882 building; the university confronted a major gap in its identity. The school's oldest building, Adelbert Hall was the campus centerpiece and a link to the past that could not be replicated. Because of its prominence, the university chose to reconstruct the sandstone structure rather than tear it down. Wisely, the goal of R.M. Kliment & Francis Halsband, Architects, was one of "interpretive reconstruction," retaining a sense of the building's original grandeur while providing a state-of-the-art facility.

The Romanesque Revival building designed by Joseph Ireland had been altered over the years, as is common. Subsequent alterations added a chapel, bookstore, and administration space to the building while compromising its appearance by adding Italianate roof braces, a reconfigured central tower, and changes in the interiors to accommodate new uses. The fire in effect erased many of the alterations by toppling the bell tower, pulling down the slate roof, and gutting the interior. Only the sandstone exterior walls and the vaulted brick and steel floor structure remained intact.

For the reconstruction, the architect reached back to that original Romanesque Revival vocabulary but chose to increase the mass and ornament of the tower. Replacement stone from the original quarry was used and the new aluminum double-glazed windows set in the same profiles and divisions as the originals. In the interior, the goal was to re-create the spirit of the grand central stairway. By enlarging the stairwell and adding new clear-glass skylights (rather than adhering to the original opaque ones), that central space became even more dramatic.

During the reconstruction, the most pressing need was to seal the building from the elements. This was accomplished by pouring a new fourth floor in concrete, leaving openings in strategic locations through which building materials could be moved down to the lower floors.

Case Western University's first building, Adelbert Hall, was ravaged by fire and then rebuilt as the campus centerpiece.

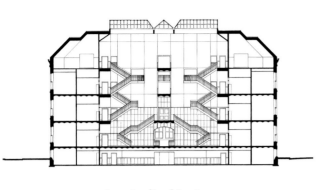

Longitudinal Section

Cross Section

On the exterior, the original Romanesque Revival style was reconstructed; in the interior, a new sky-lit stairwell was created.

WINGSPREAD

RACINE, WISCONSIN

I n the winter of 1993, an overnight ice buildup caused part of the roof of Wingspread's historic Great Hall to sag more than two inches, signaling the potentially disastrous structural failure of one of Frank Lloyd Wright's masterpieces. With ingenious team-work and a bold use of high-tech materials, the roof was strengthened and the Great Hall saved.

One of Frank Lloyd Wright's last Prairie Houses, Wingspread was designed in 1937 as the private residence for Herbert F. Johnson of the Johnson Wax family. At its center is the 430-foot-high (129-meter-high) Great Hall with a large central fireplace. Set in the elongated octagonal roof that surrounds the fireplace are 132 skylights. The remainder of the house consists of four wings extending from the Great Hall in pinwheel fashion. When the family vacated the house in 1959, it was donated to the Johnson Foundation to become a conference center.

The Hillier Group Architects, with numerous consultants, determined that while the skylights were central to Wright's design, they were also the weak link in the structural system. Wright had used only slim wooden two-by-fours to support the skylights and after decades of expansion and contraction—due to normal changes in the weather—these zigzag-shaped supports were failing. The challenge was to replace the supports without damaging the interior plaster finishes and woodwork in the Great Hall. After extensive analysis, the solution was to work from the outside in. Saving the roof tiles, which were recently added and therefore not historic, was of less concern that saving the interior finishes.

The roof of the Great Hall is composed of three sections. Staggered skylights, set on zigzag-shaped wood framing, sit between upper and lower roofs. To reinforce the wood-sheathing membrane that was stretched across the wood framing of the lower roof without adding any extra weight, boat building techniques were borrowed. The team turned to a high-strength aluminum alloy, commonly used in the aircraft industry, to tie together the upper and lower roofs. In the end, fourteen layers formed the $1/2$-inch (1-cm) shell.

The four wings of Frank Lloyd Wright's Wingspread extend outward from its octagonal core. At that core is an immense chimney crowned with rings of natural daylight. The framing members of the three rows of skylights had begun to sag and needed structural bracing.

PHOTOS: THOMAS A. HEINZ FOR THE JOHNSON FOUNDATION, INC.

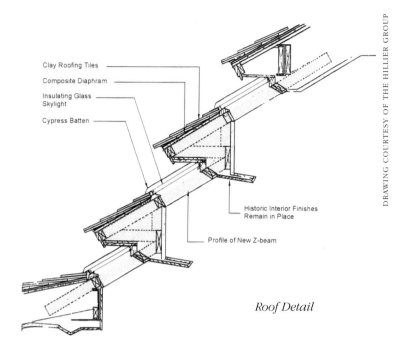

Clay Roofing Tiles

Composite Diaphram

Insulating Glass
Skylight

Cypress Batten

Historic Interior Finishes
Remain in Place

Profile of New Z-beam

Roof Detail

To correct the roof's sagging structure without destroying interior finishes, reconstruction was undertaken from outside in. Various types of shoring up were undertaken: first a temporary shoring over the roof (opposite page, top left), then a temporary enclosure erected to protect the Great Hall (opposite page, top right). When there was no fear of wind and snow loads, the building was shored up from the interior with scaffolding and then the temporary shoring removed (above left).

THE HOMER BUILDING

WASHINGTON, D.C.

Façadism is a term coined in the late 1980s to describe the practice of saving only the exterior walls of an older building and inserting new elements behind. While strict preservationists frown upon this technique, if sensitively executed, façadism can at least save a familiar streetscape that otherwise might have been lost. Take, for example, the Homer Building in the old downtown of Washington, D.C., renovated by Shalom Baranes Associates.

Ironically, research revealed that the Homer Building was originally designed by Appleton P. Clarke as a four-story structure capable of supporting five future floors. The extension was never undertaken, even though plans for adding seven floors were completed in 1926. This information eventually facilitated approval from the local landmarks board for the vertical and horizontal additions.

The first shored up the original façades, which were braced during excavation and early phases of construction with a complex structural-steel system, that, among other purposes, had to provide uninterrupted access to the subway station located at the building's base. Significant remedial work, as well as some replacement, was needed to bring the terra-cotta façades to their original appearance. The original lobby was dismantled and reassembled within the new structure as the main entry foyer.

The greatest design challenge came, however, in creating a much larger building behind the original that seamlessly continued the aesthetics established by Clarke. Using the original as a base, the architect extended upward and outward by adding finely dimensioned window niches that create a strong articulation of light and shadow. Shalom Baranes used the central entrance of the old building as a clue and, on a much larger scale, created a tripartite face whose two symmetrical wings frame a slightly recessed middle section.

While the exterior looks to the past, the interior is entirely contemporary. At its heart is a twelve-story atrium, a great public room and source of natural light. Vaulted steel trusses frame the skylight and recall the earlier use of steel spans in train stations and industrial sheds. A baroque-style stairwell tumbles from the fourth to the ground floor.

Located in the old section of downtown Washington, D.C., the Homer Building is a fine example of façadism, a practice that saves the exterior of the old while inserting spaces with much greater volume behind.

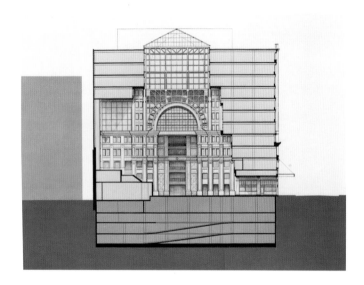

The interior is distinguished by a cavernous, twelve-story atrium that is topped by elaborate steel trusses. Donald De Lue's Spirit of American Youth *sculpture is featured.*

REHABILITATION

REHABILITATION

"The act or process of returning a property to a state of utility through repair or alteration that makes possible an efficient contemporary use while preserving those portions or features of the property that are significant to its historical, architectural, and cultural values."

U.S. SECRETARY OF
INTERIOR'S STANDARDS

ELLIS ISLAND MUSEUM

NEW YORK HARBOR

Millions of immigrants to the United States passed through the main building at Ellis Island, from which the skyline of Manhattan is now visible. The huge, barrel-vaulted Registry Room has been restored to reflect its appearance in 1918, the year the Guastavino tiles were added.

To hundreds of millions of Americans, Ellis Island symbolizes the arrival of their ancestors as immigrants to this country. Between 1892 and 1924, in the shadow of the Statue of Liberty, some 17 million new arrivals passed through the monumental main building situated on a landfill in New York Harbor. Simultaneously called a cathedral of possibilities (the passage to a new land and a new life) and place of utter fear (that you would be deported back to your homeland), this Beaux-Arts building was virtually abandoned in 1954. By the time Beyer Blinder Belle and Notter Finegold & Alexander were called in by the National Park Service to develop plans for the Ellis Island National Museum of Immigration, the monumental processing room had been compartmentalized into a warren of small rooms and offices, its beautiful tile ceiling filthy and decaying.

Now, after a faithful restoration, the huge Registry Room in which immigrants were interrogated and judged fit or unfit for entry into the United States stands as it did in 1918, the year the remarkable Guastavino tile vaults were added. Research revealed the exact positioning and style of the limestone, tile, metalwork, and plaster. The interior of the original building, designed by Boring and Tilton in 1897, was not as elaborate, yet the brick and copper exterior remains unchanged except for a new metal and glass canopy. The new canopy and dining terrace employ crisp materials that are intentionally different in texture from the original elements of the building.

It is the 160-foot-long (48-meter-long), two-story Registry Room that evokes the great-est emotion and it was quite appropriate—and unusual—that the Park Service and the architects decided to present this room and the baggage area as exhibitions unto themselves rather than as containers of other exhibitions. The smaller exhibition rooms are in the building's wings. To get to the museum, visitors follow the exact path from the baggage room through the Registry Room that the immigrants did long ago.

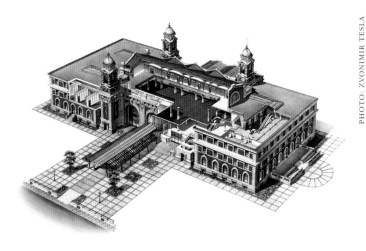

The new metal and glass canopy intentionally contrasts with the original Beaux-Arts design. From it, the Statue of Liberty is visible. While the main Registry Room was preserved to its 1918 appearance, ancillary rooms and passageways have been adapted to meet contemporary needs, such as the sky-lit escalator (opposite, below).

Immigrants would enter the
Registry Room up stairs
from the baggage room
before, a path visitors now
use to enter the Ellis Island
museum.

The unique weave pattern
of the tiles on the barrel
vaults in the Registry Room
was replicated, as was the
design of the original
chandeliers.

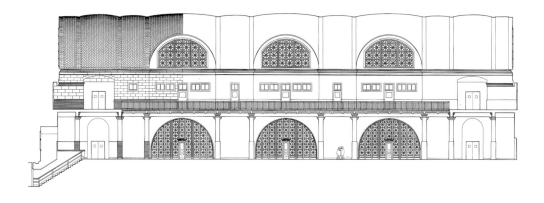

FLEET BANK

ALBANY, NEW YORK

The adaptive use of abandoned heroic landmark buildings can pose a delicate problem. How can a virtually obsolete, yet huge, space be altered for new use without destroying its architectural integrity? A superb example is the Fleet Bank Corporate Headquarters and Data Service Center, once Albany's Union Station, a grand monument to rail travel. Renovated by Einhorn Yaffee Prescott, it now stands as a testimony to the possibilities of design ingenuity.

Designed by Shepley Rutan & Coolidge and completed in 1900, Union Station thrived until the 1950s, when the age of superhighways and flight drained its life away. Although listed on the National Register of Historic Places, this Beaux-Arts station was abandoned and vandalized. So complete was its deterioration that trees were growing on the roof, its walls and 52-foot-high (15.8-meter-high) ceiling were falling, and its steel and granite frame was disintegrating. In the late 1970s the governor of New York saved the station with a million-dollar weatherproofing, yet the building remained vacant. It would be another decade before Fleet Bank (then Norstar Bancorp) purchased the building—but only on the condition that the usable floor space be doubled from 50,000 to 100,000 square feet (4,645 to 9,290 square meters) while maintaining the building's original architectural spirit and fabric.

The solution was to reduce the four-story, monumental concourse to three stories. This meant moving the original cast-iron façades, which originally were 10 feet (3 meters) from the wall, inward 20 feet (6.1 meters), and creating another mezzanine level. In the process, the first floor became a highly secure computer nerve center for the bank. The restoration of interior surfaces was extensive, such as molding plaster pieces from remaining ones and restoring the fluted columns, ornate railings, glass panels, and decorative ornamentation found on the cast-iron façades. Threading modern communications, electrical, mechanical, and security systems into the building without destroying its historical integrity was a major technical challenge.

Infusing new life into Union Station has brought renewed activity to this area of Albany. Fleet Bank and Einhorn Yaffee Prescott are to be congratulated.

PHOTO: COURTESY OF EINHORN YAFFEE PRESCOTT

The once prominent Union Station had become a monumental mausoleum until it was saved from demolition by Fleet Bank. Now, although the usable interior space has been doubled, the interior reflects much of its former glory.

PHOTO: BILL MURPHY

69

The proportions of the grand concourse were preserved in the renovation while reducing the great room from four to three stories. Restoration of the interior surfaces was extensive and painstaking. New functions were inserted into previously open spaces, such as the executive office reception area.

Corporate Offices

Before

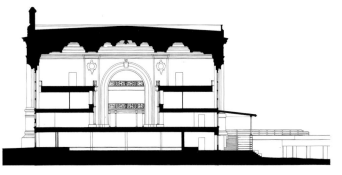

After

The canopy that once sheltered patrons boarding trains in the rear of the station was replicated as a covered pedestrian walkway to the nearby garage.

MISSION INN

RIVERSIDE, CALIFORNIA

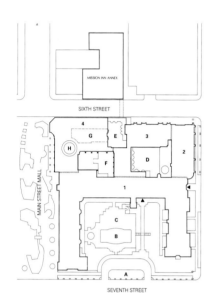

At the dawn of the twentieth century, the Mission Inn rose in Riverside, California, through the persistence of an entrepreneur named Frank Miller. A devotee of Spanish architecture, Miller over nearly thirty years created a unique hotel. With his death in 1935, the hotel slid into a state of disrepair and decline, and remained virtually abandoned until renovation began in 1984. With the expertise of ELS/Elbansi & Logan Architects of Berkeley, California, the hotel has reopened and is once again a thriving resort destination.

The 320,000-square-foot (28,800-square-meter), 240-guest room Mission Inn occupies an entire block in downtown Riverside. Because it was built in four stages between 1903 and 1931, the construction techniques varied, as did the renovation requirements. Most in need of seismic upgrading was the 1903 Mission Wing. Renovation of this wing required the replacement of several layers of brick with reinforced concrete or reinforcing steel rods. The walls were then plastered to match the original. Unbolted hollow cast-iron columns supporting the western façade were replaced with steel columns, which in turn were anchored firmly to an underground concrete beam running the length of the wing. In the east wing, new steel beams and steel columns were installed within existing stud walls to support sagging corridors and ceiling beams.

A less extensive renovation of the three other wings was required and consisted of a careful restoration of finishes and systems upgrades. The Cloister Wing took its inspiration from historic Spanish missions found elsewhere in California. The Spanish Wing, built in 1913 and 1914, was directly influenced by Miller's extended travels in Spain. In these two wings, nonbearing walls were reinforced and unpainted plaster repaired to match the original. The Rotunda Wing, completed in 1931, combines Spanish motifs with oriental design. Visitors are welcomed into the hotel through two rebuilt arches.

The view down the multi-story, stair-encircled Rotunda is quite dramatic. Visitors are welcomed through one of the two reconstructed Mission-style arches.

PHOTO: ERICH KOYAMA

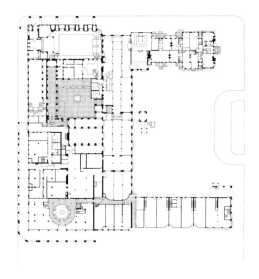

A grand staircase marks the renovated lobby.

PHOTO: TIMOTHY HURSLEY

The massive Inn was built in four different stages over thirty years and consists of several design motifs—Mission-style, Spanish, and Oriental.

An intimate courtyard fronts the chapel.

PRESERVATION PARK DISTRICT

OAKLAND, CALIFORNIA

I t is not unusual today for entire complexes of Victorian-style houses to spring up overnight. It *is* surprising, though, when the new development actually consists of genuine Victorian houses originating from the 1880s to 1900. Welcome to Preservation Park, a four-block area containing sixteen Victorian houses adapted for office use. What makes Preservation Park unusual is that only five of these houses were previously located on site. The eleven other houses were in nearby communities and facing imminent demolition. Each was carefully moved under the vigilant eye of the Architectural Resources Group to Preservation Park, steps away from the Oakland City Hall.

When all the houses were in place, each was meticulously restored to its original exterior appearance, while the interiors were adapted for office use. In the adaptation, the interior volumes and historic details were retained. Extensive landscaping makes Preservation Park an almost idyllic streetscape; one almost expects to see horse-drawn carriages. The main parking lot is sensitively hidden behind a grouping of homes. A raised walkway, with ramp access, links the upper floors of several buildings, providing maximum access for visitors who are disabled.

At the center of Preservation Park is the Nile Club Assembly Hall, which was added to the Frederick Ginn House in 1911. The assembly hall was used mainly by a men's social organizations for meetings, performances, and dinners until it was abandoned in the 1920s. Now renovated by the Architectural Resources Group, with acoustical and theater consultants, the club houses a 300-seat auditorium.

The sixteen Victorian houses that make up Preservation Park have been meticulously restored. Of the sixteen, eleven were moved from other sites. At the heart of the complex is the Nile Club, restored as a 300-seat auditorium (above).

The site plan of Preservation Park reveals how deliberately each house was placed along its new street and a parking lot hidden behind a grouping of houses.

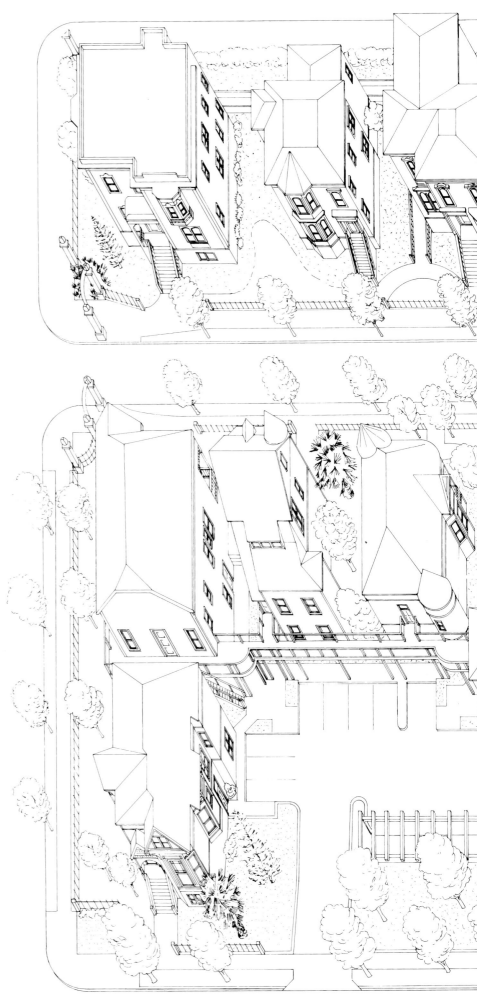

SHERATON PALACE HOTEL

SAN FRANCISCO, CALIFORNIA

When the Sheraton Palace opened its doors in 1875 as the largest hotel of its time, it quickly gained the reputation as the most opulent hotel west of the Mississippi. Even a horrific fire in 1906 didn't close the hotel down. It was rebuilt and, again, soon became the focal point of San Francisco high society. In this renovation, the former Grand Court, where passengers once alighted from horse-drawn carriages, was covered with a leaded-glass, domed ceiling to become the elegant, three-story-tall Garden Court. But the cycle of renewal and decline affects even the grandest and by the late 1980s, the hotel was shabby, its building systems obsolete. The Loma Prieta Earthquake in 1989 underscored the need for seismic upgrading.

Undertaken by Skidmore, Owings & Merrill, the Garden Court was meticulously restored to its 1909 appearance. The rest of the hotel, however, was sensitively modernized to incorporate the latest mechanical and life-safety systems and to bring to the hotel a late-twentieth-century ambience. In renovating the lobby, other public areas, and the health spa, SOM echoed the Garden Court's form in new vaulted ceilings that provide a contemporary elegance to the hotel.

The restored Garden Court reflects its original refined elegance. The lead and glass domed ceiling became the form maker for the major spaces in the hotel, such as the main lobby, a seating area, and the pool, all of which are huge, vaulted areas.

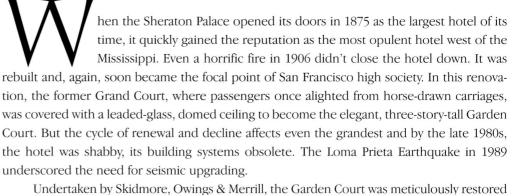

U.S. DISTRICT COURT OF APPEALS

SAN FRANCISCO, CALIFORNIA

This grand Beaux-Arts building received a seismic upgrading using base-isolation technology during its renovation, which will more likely secure its existence through future earthquakes. Opulent barrel-vaulted hallways run throughout the building.

The 1989 Loma Prieta earthquake that ravaged parts of Northern California raised the stakes on historic buildings there. Many suffered severe structural damage, like the 1905 U.S. District Court of Appeals, which experienced extensive cracking of the interior's hollow clay tiles and the exterior's unreinforced granite blocks. It made sense, then, for the U.S. General Services Administration (the federal government's building management agency) to undertake seismic upgrading as it proceeded with the renovation of the classical building under the guidance of Skidmore, Owings & Merrill. The program called for the conversion of the building from a post office/courthouse to a complex for the U.S. Court of Appeals.

Called one of the most opulent public buildings west of the Mississippi, the 350,000-square-foot (31,500-square-meter) building was designed by James Knox Taylor. In this Beaux-Arts treasure, marble mosaics decorate the barrel-vaulted suspended ceilings. Elaborate plaster moldings, marble wainscot panels, mosaic tiles, and intricate wood panels overlay hollow clay tile. In the restoration, these surfaces were brought back to their original sparkle, even while modern building services were inserted. The former two-story light court was redesigned in a contemporary idiom as a two-story atrium and mezzanine structure, in the process increasing usable space by 45,000 square feet (4,181 square meters).

To seismically upgrade the structure, the architects turned to base-isolation technology, which at that time was considered highly innovative. This type of retrofit minimally altered the important historic spaces and features and actually reduced the amount of work required to reinforce the 300-foot (90-meter) dome. Most of the seismic work occurred in the basement, thus calling for little reinforcement in the upper levels. A new steel-framed metal deck was inserted at the ground floor to reduce the floor-to-ceiling height after 250 friction-pendulum isolators were installed under each structural column.

The style of courtrooms ranges from Victorian (below) to a 1930s Art Deco (left).

To increase usable interior space, the architect inserted a new atrium and mezzanine structure into the former light court and made it distinctively contemporary in style.

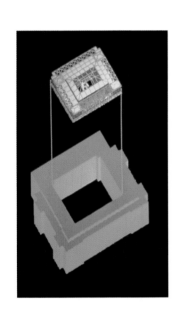

SANTA ROSA RAILROAD DEPOT

SANTA ROSA, CALIFORNIA

Preservation of an individual building can be a catalyst to renewal of others. Such is the intention in Santa Rosa, where city government officials elected to renovate the historic railroad depot to promote revitalization of the city's Railroad Square Historic District. The long-term goal is for the depot to be used as a multimodal transportation center; in the interim the building, renovated by Glenn David Mathews, AIA, serves as a visitor center.

The Santa Rosa Railroad Depot was built in 1904 as a station on the Northwestern Pacific Railroad line. Passenger service was curtailed in 1958, and the building, made of local basalt stone and redwood timbers, was vacated and left to deteriorate. Today it is one of the few remaining stone railroad depots in the West, and a lovely, compact one at that. Architect Mathews found seismic upgrading to be the most critical aspect of the renovation—that is, making the building safer in the event of an earthquake without compromising the building's historic integrity.

Rather than using conventional X-bracing in the interior, Mathews devised an innovative lateral resistance system composed of three elements. The first is a containment wall attached to the interior side of the perimeter stone wall and pony wall, with plywood shear panels nailed to the inside surface to stiffen the building's resistance to lateral movement. The second is a system of two plywood diaphragms, one installed over the interior of the depot at the ceiling level and the other located above the loggia ceiling. The third element is the installation of rigid steel columns inside two of the stone loggia columns. The solution resulted in interior walls eight inches thicker than the original but with no detectable visual difference.

The rest of the building was carefully restored, yet scars on the stone walls made over the years by the baggage cars were retained as a reminder of past times.

A stop of the Northwestern Pacific Railroad line, the Santa Rosa Depot suffered with the decline of rail service. Newly renovated, it sits as the showplace of the city's Railroad Square Historic District. A conference room has been inserted into the former baggage room.

The architect elected to meticulously restore the basalt stone and redwood timber depot while retaining visual signs of its past, such as baggage scars in the stone. The interior now houses a local visitor center.

DUMBARTON OAKS

WASHINGTON, D.C.

The new gallery was inserted into a previously inaccessible courtyard. On the exterior, its form borrows from existing building elements.

Over time, sensitively executed renovations and additions can bring more splendor to already palatial estates. Dumbarton Oaks is an example. Set on an exquisitely landscaped, sloping property in the northern portion of Washington's Georgetown section, the latest addition to the mansion is a 10,000-square-foot (900-square-meter) gallery set into a previously inaccessible outdoor courtyard. For the design of that room, Hartman-Cox Architects was inspired by the classical idiom of the other portions of the house, particularly the renowned McKim, Mead, and White 1929 music room. The result is a small jewel placed in a much larger, glittering ensemble.

To truly appreciate the new gallery at Dumbarton Oaks, one must understand the somewhat eclectic history of the estate's development. Built in 1800 as a Federalist-style farmhouse, the structure was Victorianized in the mid-nineteenth century with the addition of a mansard roof, octagonal tower, and cupola. By the 1920s it was a rundown villa of rambling porches and balconies surrounded by an overgrown garden. In 1920 the estate was bought by a career diplomat and his wife, the Robert Wood Blisses, who in the next twenty years amassed a substantial collection of American Indian art as well as Byzantine and Hellenistic relics. In 1940 the Blisses gave the estate to Harvard University after completely reconstructing the original mansion and its gardens. In 1963 a museum of pre-Columbian art, designed by Philip Johnson, was added to the estate.

The Hartman-Cox gallery looks back to the original ambience of the mansion rather than aligning itself with the modernism of the Johnson addition. The new gallery is edged on three sides by a colonnaded passageway with paired Ionic columns matching those found in the McKim, Mead, and White music room. A focal point in the gallery is the Palladian window, which is shared by the music room. Unlike other parts of the house, however, the gallery is suffused with natural light from a glazed opening in its barrel-vaulted ceiling. The renovation also led to improved security by separating research and staff areas from public spaces, enlarging the entry vestibule, clarifying interior circulation, and adding new underground mechanical areas, storage, and library stacks.

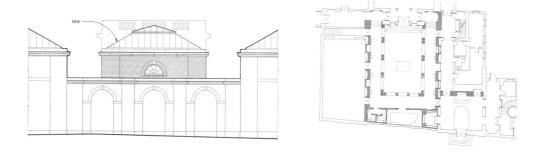

The gallery receives an abundance of natural light from the glazed windows set into its barrel-vaulted ceiling. Paired Ionic columns visually separate the main portion of the room and the perimeter hallway. The adjoining McKim, Mead, and White music room (right) inspired the design of the gallery.

AMSTEL HOTEL

AMSTERDAM, THE NETHERLANDS

The Grand Hall was meticulously restored to its 1866 majesty. Located in the heart of the city, the newly restored hotel boasts a Second French Empire appearance with its eclectic mixture of architectural details.

I n Amsterdam, a grand European hotel became even grander through its renovation by RKTL and Erik Lopes Cardozo. Located on the Amstel River in the heart of Amsterdam, the splendid, landmark nineteenth-century hotel had been tarnished by age. In fact, the 1866 vintage hotel required structural improvements as well as restoration of the brick, timber, and stone façade. Now renovated, its exterior is a stately early Second Empire presence, with mansard roofs and somewhat eclectic combination of window styles, cupolas, and details.

Inside, however, the hotel is quite classical in details and ambience. The grand public rooms, such as the Grand Hall and the ballroom, were meticulously restored. To maintain the elegance and integrity of the original interior surfaces, state-of-the-art electrical and mechanical systems were delicately inserted. The hotel's 111 tiered guest rooms were transformed into seventy-nine five-star accommodations.

A major challenge in the renovation of an older hotel is providing space for contemporary services. To do so, the architects demolished an unsympathetic 1960s extension set along the river front and replaced it with a brick and precast stone addition topped with a classically designed conservatory. The new addition houses a ninety-seven-seat restaurant and a leisure center with a swimming pool, health club, and spa facilities. The conservatory acts as a terrace opening to the outdoors and views of the river.

Maintaining a magnificent presence along the Amstel River, an addition topped by a classical-style conservatory offers contemporary amenities to the hotel, such as the swimming pool, expanded dining facilities, and other interior spaces that extend the elegant ambience of the Grand Hall.

SAINT ANDREWS OLD COURSE HOTEL

SAINT ANDREWS, SCOTLAND

The desire to perpetuate the character of a place through sympathetic design of its new buildings was a notion disregarded by the modern movement in architecture. It is, however, an ethic that has returned, and nowhere is that more evident than in the renovation of the Saint Andrews Old Course Hotel. Constructed in 1960, its exterior walls were of a stark concrete, a nondescript image within view of the grand historic Saint Andrews Hotel. The appearance of the 1960s hotel has now been brought back in line with the older hotel and, according to RTKL, Associates, Inc., architect of the project, now "exudes an elegance befitting the birthplace of golf five centuries ago."

The goal was to bring the 1960s hotel visually in line with the historic Saint Andrews. The architect, therefore, added a pitched slate roof, wrought-iron balconies, French doors, glazing with traditional Scottish detailing, and cast-stone cornices. The band concrete exterior walls were redone in harl, a centuries-old traditional Scottish building finish. Foliage was used to soften the stone-walled motor court that leads guests to a glass porte cochere and sky-lit entry. Another requirement was to expand the hotel. In doing so, the architect chose forms and fenestration matching the appearance of the renovated hotel.

In the richly appointed interiors, the ground-floor corridors were relocated to the golf course side. Rooms were realigned to take maximum advantage of vistas of the course, the North Sea, and the neighboring town. Modern amenities were provided through the enlargement and remodeling of a 8,000-square-foot (720-square-meter) spa, the construction of a lap pool enclosed by a glass-domed pavilion, the renovation of the pro shop, and the addition of a 30,000-square-foot (2,700-square-meter) ballroom/meeting room.

The renovation of Saint Andrews aligns the image of the 1960s hotel more closely with that of the golf course's historic buildings. The hotel overlooks the seventeenth hole, or "Road Hole," of the fabled Saint Andrews Old Course.

ALL PHOTOS: SCOTT MCDONALD © HEDRICH BLESSING

The hotel's interiors are exquisitely appointed, with extensive woodworking, as seen in the lobby. Other interior spaces include the conservatory, library, skylight courtyard, and dining room.

The two wings added to the
1960s structure extend the
renovated hotel's image
through the use of similar
materials and fenestration.
The pool house and the
entrance sport clear-glazed
roofs.

MARSH AND MCLENNAN BUILDING

BALTIMORE, MARYLAND

A proud survivor of Baltimore's Fire of 1904, this office and warehouse boasts one of the city's three remaining cast-iron façades. By the late 1980s, however, it faced extinction. Although listed on the U.S. National Register of Historic Places and exhibiting a degree of ornamentation rare in cast-iron structures, its economic viability was threatened in an urban environment thriving with much larger and more modern buildings. In the end, its rebirth as the Marsh and McLennan Building involved a delicate juggling act of restoration, adaptation, and addition by RTKL Associates, Inc.

City zoning rules call for new construction in this part of town to be set back 50 feet (15.2 meters). This significantly affected the relationship between the new and old elements, allowing the cast-iron Northern Italian Renaissance Revival façade to remain prominent. As a remembrance of the past, part of the exposed western side of the original building is covered in granite to create the ghost appearance of a once adjacent three-story building.

The addition surrounds the back half of the original five-story, six-bay structure. What makes the project aesthetically successful was RTKL's ability to create a unified architectural statement in which the new does not cartoon the prominent original architectural elements but instead employs sympathetic massing. The architect chose an aluminum brise-soleil front that reinterprets the depth and repetitive detailing of the original's cast-iron arches and entablatures. In effect, the newly created glass modules appear as a modern, rhythmic repetition of the old.

Great care was taken to return the cast-iron façade to its original appearance, with missing sections recast. However, to adapt the 1904 building for a contemporary office, extensive internal changes were necessary. While the two load-bearing walls needed only to be cleaned and repointed, the mezzanines were removed. The entire roof structure was replaced with steel. Many of the historic features, like metal fire shutters and sets of rolling fire doors separating the east and west sections of every floor, were restored, using original materials if possible.

RESTORED CAST IRON FACADE
SCALE   1/4" = 1'-0"

Embraced at its rear by a glassy addition, the original, highly decorative cast-iron façade is softly lit at night.

PHOTOS: SCOTT MCDONALD © HEDRICH BLESSING

By nearly doubling the square footage of the original building, the addition presents a modern backdrop, with its brise-soleil window design sympathetically echoing the original's cast-iron bays. Granite panels on the east side of the original building hint at the historic storefront context.

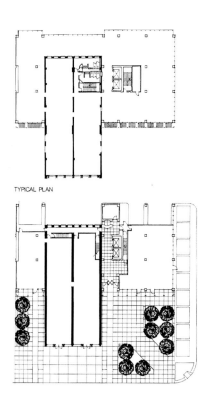

TYPICAL PLAN

The restored lobby of the old and the updated lobby of the addition celebrate different moods. On the exterior, the relationship between old and new is highly sympathetic.

PARLIN MEMORIAL LIBRARY

EVERETT, MASSACHUSETTS

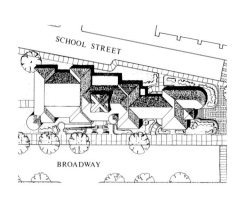

Built in 1895, the 8,000-square-foot (720-square-meter) Richardsonian Romanesque Revival–style Parlin Memorial Library served the town of Everett well—that is, for the first eighty years or so, until the needs of library users had outgrown the physical space. Gradually, over time, its once elegant interiors, complete with two fireplaces, free-standing fluted columns, and dark oak woodwork, was buried under or behind book stacks or reading chairs. The opportunity to win a state grant to expand the library couldn't have come at a better time. For help with the grant application, the town turned to the architecture firm of Childs Bertman Tseckares Inc. to develop a plan to more than double the size of the existing building. The solution was a contextual plan in which the addition sympathetically borrowed from the existing building, creating a much larger library that expanded the heritage of the original as well as its size.

The addition blends so well with the original that at first glance it is hard to distinguish old from new. This was accomplished by echoing the rounded corners and towers, flow lines, and articulated spaces of the original building. When one looks closely, differences *can* be detected, due mainly to a reinterpretation of materials. Instead of the original horizontal banding of the stone base, the architect chose precast concrete for the lower portion of the façade. A second color of precast on the upper levels visually responds to the existing terra-cotta. The buff-colored brick was carefully matched. The greatest difference is the checkerboard pattern of earth-toned brick that stretches across the new façade under the roofline and is repeated on the new tower. This pattern is also used inside to mark the new lobby.

Adding 12,000 square feet (1,115 square meters) in effect freed the interior of the old library to be restored to its former glory. The overall interior plan is now simplified as one linear spine on each floor extending the length of the building.

As seen from the front, the addition sits sympathetically next to the original building on the left.

By the more than doubling of the size of the original library, clutter obscuring the elegant details could be removed. The main entrance was shifted to the addition and is marked by a new monumental stair on the exterior and a new lobby inside.

LOS ANGELES CENTRAL LIBRARY

LOS ANGELES, CALIFORNIA

The decision to save this distinctive Goodhue-designed central library marked a turning point for the city of Los Angeles: It bucked the trend to ever-expanding sprawl. The library, it was decided after a debate that lasted nearly two decades, would remain the city's main branch and lure patrons downtown. In the end the city prospered not only from the library's restoration and an addition that nearly doubled the original building's capacity but also from the re-creation of a delightful public garden. The project was a task of many parts undertaken by a team of historians and art experts and craftsmen, accomplished under the guiding hand of Hardy Holzman Pfeiffer Associates.

Designed by Bertram Grosvenor Goodhue and opened in 1926, stylistically the Los Angeles Central Library was an eclectic mix of Spanish colonial, Byzantine, and Art Moderne that quickly became a landmark downtown. Yet, over the years, as the library's holdings and the demand for its services grew, the original splendor was tarnished and in some cases literally obscured.

Early on, the architect determined that the Goodhue building must be restored as closely as possible to its original appearance and that the addition must defer to it. The central rotunda with its tapestry-like murals is now a ceremonial hall. The original reading rooms have been converted into the children's section. The exclamation point of the exterior is once again the brilliantly colored pyramidal tower.

With a cross-shaped floor plan, the Goodhue building was designed to stand alone. Connecting that building to a large addition yet not diminishing the Goodhue design was a major design challenge. In the architect's scheme, the new defers to the old, but is definitely a contemporary design. Inside, a glass-covered atrium rises eight stories. To camouflage the bulk, nearly one half of the atrium is set below the ground. Surrounding the atrium are new reading rooms and stacks.

Set among skyscrapers, the brilliantly colored pyramidal tower of the library remains a strong urban presence. The façade is decorated with lavish limestone carvings.

PHOTOS: FOAAD FARAH

The lush murals and stenciling in the Goodhue interiors were meticulously restored to their original appearance, a brilliance that had been obscured over time by overcrowdedness and fire damage. The central rotunda is now a ceremonial hall.

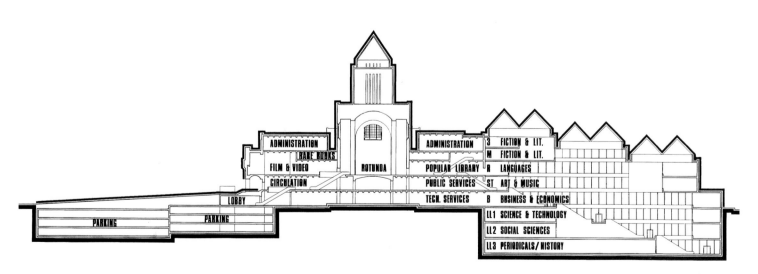

The addition sits congenially beside the Goodhue library, taking cues from the original building but presenting them in a very contemporary mode. The Maguire Gardens reestablished the library's historic west lawn, now a delightful public amenity.

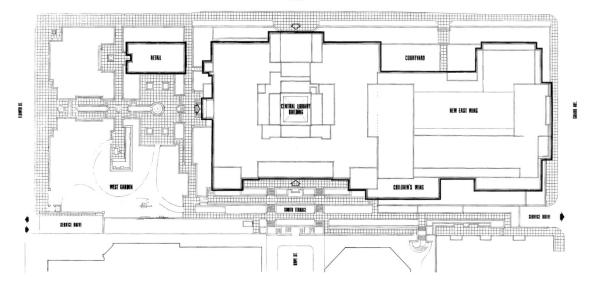

LOS ANGELES CENTRAL LIBRARY 121

The addition's eight-story atrium is partially underground. It is a space full of natural light with escalators that tumble down like a waterfall. Reading rooms and stacks are positioned on each side of the atrium.

ROSS COMMONS

MIDDLEBURY COLLEGE, MIDDLEBURY, VERMONT

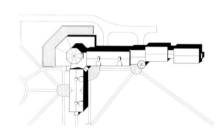

At Middlebury College, a group of four modern residential halls were out of place among the more Collegiate Gothic buildings on campus. In fact, many thought the complex an eyesore, a rude intrusion on an otherwise lovely, traditional campus. Internally, the dormitories were outdated and did not meet students' expectations of privacy or comfort, yet, the buildings' core of reinforced concrete walls, attached to a concrete frame and set on bedrock, was structurally sound. Rather than tearing down the complex—known as the Milliken, Hadley, Kelly, and Lang Residence Halls—Einhorn Yaffee Prescott chose to save the structural framework while gutting the buildings, reorganizing their floor plans, connecting them, and adding more common space. Most significant, from an aesthetic standpoint, was the decision to reclad the complex in materials that reinforced the architectural heritage of the campus.

The choice of cladding material was all-important. Because the local limestone used elsewhere on campus was no longer available, a Corinthian granite was chosen for its lively range of colors. A pinkish Stony Creek granite was used as a contrast at the lintels and sills.

In the renovation of Ross Lounge, a tower was added above the original building and clad in white clapboard to reflect the generic design of silos found in the nearby Vermont countryside. The tower image was repeated at a smaller scale—and this time clad in granite—at the link between Kelly/Lang on one side and Hadley on the other. Internally, the floors were arranged in a new horizontal alignment.

The restoration of this complex of four dormitories and social hall took an unusual direction: the exterior surface, considered an eyesore, was removed and replaced by materials more in sympathy with the campus tradition. The newly added tower picked up the vernacular language of the Vermont countryside.

SCHLUMBERGER FACTORY

MONTROUGE, FRANCE

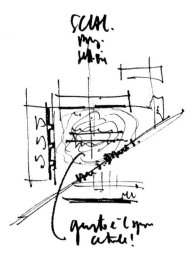

With the renovation of the Schlumberger Factory, the company's twenty-year transformation from a manufacturer of electromechanics to electronics was completed. As the grittiness went out of the manufacturing process, so, too, did the physical environment change from a bleak collection of factory buildings into a new complex boasting a large public park. This transformation occurred under the guiding hand of Renzo Piano Building Workshop with Ove Arup and Partners.

In the renovation the sixteen five-story factory buildings were modernized, yet the façade's geometric pattern was retained. They now stand as reminders of the past but also look toward the future. A single-story building at the site's center was demolished and in its place a 6,000-square-feet (20,000-square-meter) garden was created. The garden is unusual in that underneath part of it is parking for 1,000 cars. More significantly, the ground was mounded over a restaurant, bar, bank, travel agency, sports facility, auditorium, projects room, conference room, and the administration headquarters. These areas are accessed down a passageway covered with a tent structure that is a dominant visual element in the public garden.

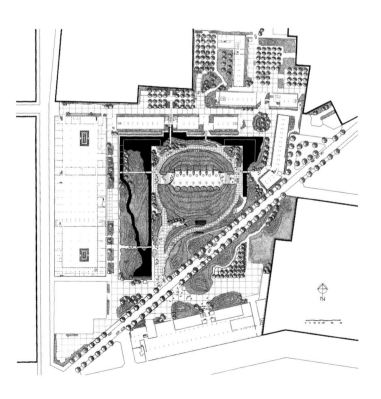

Through the factory's renovation, Renzo Piano sought to heighten the geometry of the original buildings but at the same time introduce a natural garden as a unifying element.

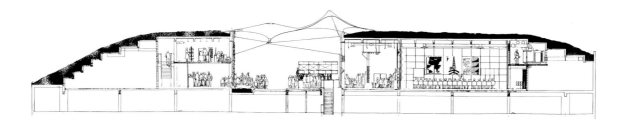

A single-story building was demolished to make room for the large garden. At its heart a tent structure shields pedestrian access to commercial activities such as shops, restaurants, and conference facilities.

PHOTO: M. DENANCE

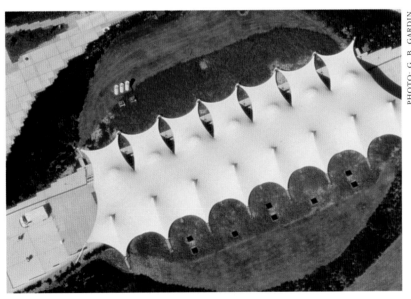

PHOTO: G. B. GARDIN

ADAPTIVE USE

ADAPTIVE USE

"The process of converting a building to a use other than that for which it was designed, e.g., changing a factory into housing. Such conversions are accomplished with varying alterations to the building."

THE NATIONAL TRUST FOR HISTORIC PRESERVATION

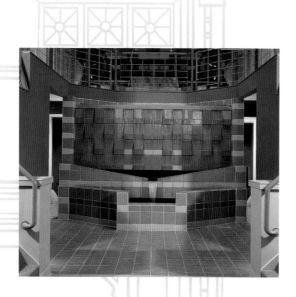

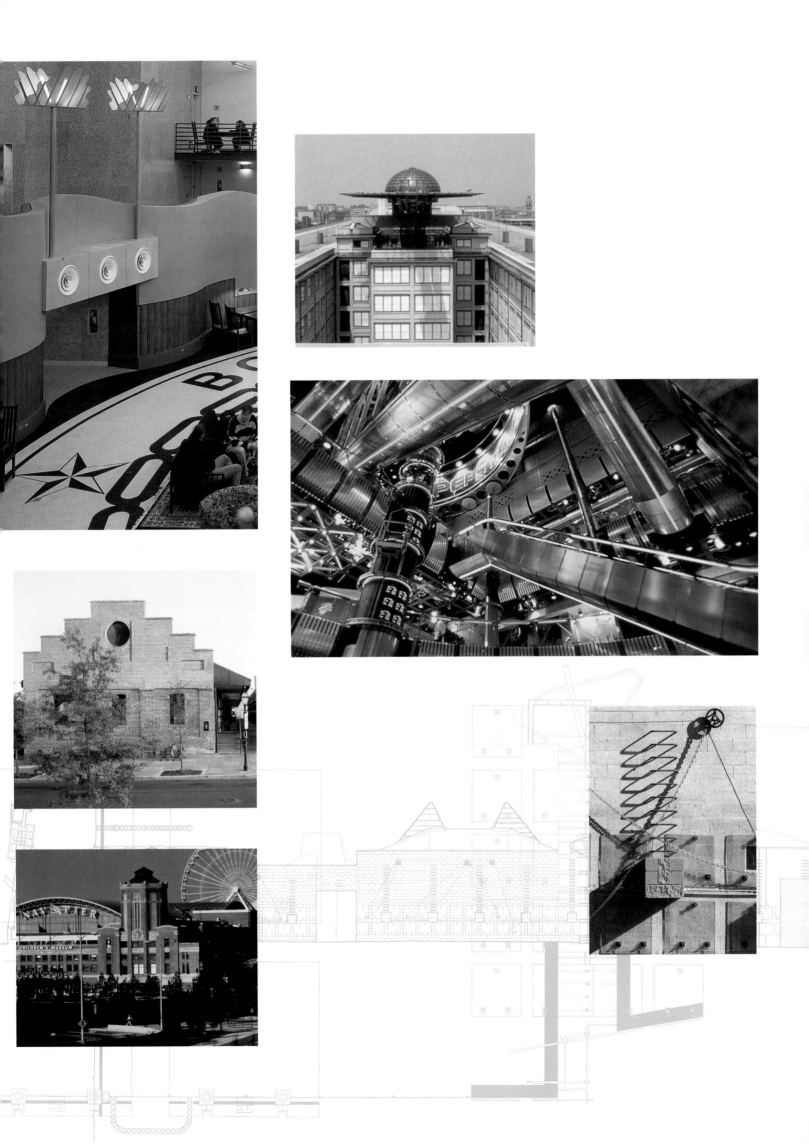

MASSACHUSETTS WATER RESOURCES AUTHORITY

BOSTON, MASSACHUSETTS

Surrounded and dwarfed by new water treatment facilities on an island in Boston Harbor, the once abandoned turn-of-the-century sewage pumping station has become, in its renewed state, a focal point of the entire modern-day complex as the reception and training building. Not only has the pump been retained as a symbol of what was once a marvel of engineering but also the building serves as a state-of-the-art training center for Water Resources Authority employees. All was accomplished by Tsoi/Kobus & Associates, Architects, through extensive research in an effort to preserve the original architectural character of the 18,400-square-foot (1,656-square-meter) station while meeting current building criteria.

The most extensive change provided a large, flexible space for the training and conference area. This was accomplished by combining two narrow wings under a new hip roof while maintaining the original exterior roofline. Slate on the roof was matched from the Vermont quarry from which the original was taken. The cupola was also renewed through a search for the original materials. Skilled craftsmen faithfully restored the terra-cotta trim on the roof ridges and hips. Although not part of the original structure, the badly deteriorated 125-foot-high (37.5-meter-high) exhaust stack was renovated for its sentimental value as a visual symbol of the island.

The renewed turn-of-the-century sewage pumping station stands as a reminder of New England's proud architectural and engineering heritage.

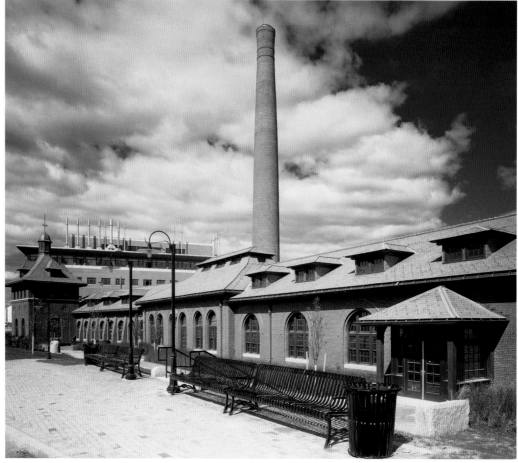

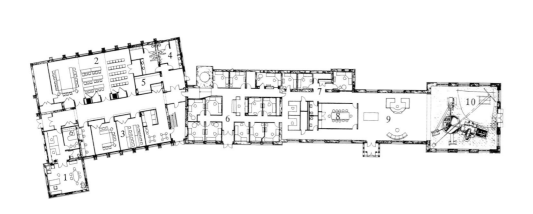

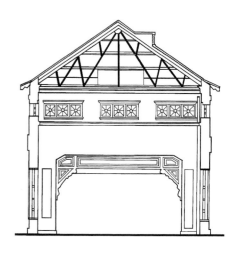

The restored original pump is the focal point for visitors to this renowned waste-water treatment plant. A large training area for treatment plant employees is supplemented by a small conference room that overlooks the historic pump.

TINDECO WHARF

BALTIMORE, MARYLAND

During the past century, as our industrial-dominated society has been transformed by high technology, the character of entire cities has changed. This is exemplified by Baltimore, Maryland. Located at the northern reaches of the Chesapeake Bay, the city grew strong as an industrial port city, yet by the last quarter of the twentieth century its inner harbor was virtually abandoned. Intervention of the city and a far-sighted developer brought new life to the harbor with a gleaming retail and restaurant complex. That complex, known as Harbor Place, in turn sparked an examination of the old industrial structures lining the bay, such as the former Tin Decorating Company manufacturing plant. Its reuse as luxury housing, as designed by Cho, Wilks & Benn, has extended the redevelopment of the harbor.

Fronting the Fells Point/Canton Historic District, the huge, four-story brick building was constructed in 1914. At the height of its operations, the Tin Decorating Company employed 2,800 people and produced four million tin Tindeco containers each day. Its rebirth was prompted by a growing demand for in-town waterfront apartments. The new mixed-use development offers twenty-four rental residential units as well as 38,000 square feet (3,530 square meters) of commercial and retail space.

The apartments are airy and light-filled lofts with oversized windows, 14- to 20-foot (4.3- to 6.1-meter) ceiling heights, and original wood ceilings and brick walls. Every unit receives abundant natural light as the building is punctured in its center by a 106-by-168-foot (32-by-50-meter) courtyard. Overlooking this newly landscaped court are twenty-two penthouse units as well as a common roof promenade. A wise decision was made to retain the brick powerhouse and its 110-foot-high (33-meter-high) smokestack as a restaurant. Its surrounding pier is a park, pool area, promenade, and marina for the entire Tindeco complex.

Now luxury housing, the four-story former Tin Decorating Company manufacturing plant is fronted by the powerhouse-turned-restaurant, a green space, and a pool.

A spectacular atrium runs through the heart of the old manufacturing plant and serves as an entrance to the housing as well as the retail and commercial areas.

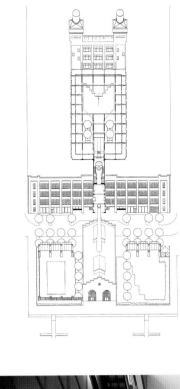

Penthouse apartments and a common promenade overlook the central courtyard. The landscaping design focuses on a fountain, the water of which moves into the building and through its lower lobby.

MERCY FAMILY PLAZA

SAN FRANCISCO, CALIFORNIA

The former hospital complex is surrounded by colorful Victorian houses. The four units converted into affordable housing line the complex's northern edge. Exteriors were carefully preserved; interiors were gutted and redesigned.

As the demand for privately sponsored affordable housing grew in the United States during the past decade, so did the creative reuse of historic buildings for this purpose. One brilliant example is the Mercy Family Plaza in San Francisco, where four buildings of a former hospital complex were converted to affordable housing. In doing so, Sandy & Babcock successfully faced the challenge of creating appropriate housing under a stringent budget while adhering to federal and local guidelines for renovating historic buildings.

Located one block from Golden Gate Park in a neighborhood of Victorian-era town-houses, the neoclassical hospital complex was built by the Southern Pacific Railroad between 1907 and 1930. Operations ceased in 1973 and the hospital lay vacant for a decade until the Sisters of Mercy began the renovation of the main hospital building into Mercy Terrace, a housing complex for the elderly. An additional 33,000 square feet (3,066 square meters) of building space remained vacant until the plan for affordable housing was approved.

The easiest building to convert proved to be the nurses' annex, which now houses twenty-six of the thirty-six units; the most difficult was the powerhouse. There the architect inserted a new floor system over the original boiler pit to create eight loft apartments. The powerhouse features 12-foot-high (3.7-meter-high) double-hung windows, yet parts of the interior suffered from lack of natural light, a situation corrected by the addition of skylights. More challenging was the historic preservation board's requirement that the arched windows remain undisturbed. Instead of bringing the new second-floor slab directly up to the exterior wall at the window, the architect devised a system of metal grates that function like drawbridges. In the nurses' annex, the architect cut away the floors and built new structural walls consisting of a reinforcing-steel frame covered with gunite. The social hall was gutted, except for the original terrazzo and tile entry stair, and reshaped into four large apartments. The fourth building, the small one-story utility building adjacent to the nurses' annex, was converted to a recreation room with kitchenette.

Viewed by the Landmarks Board as a "character-defining element," the powerhouse smokestack was seismically reinforced. The powerhouse is also identified by its 12-foot-high (3.7-meter-high) arched windows. The four-story nurses' annex and two-story social hall march down the hill from the powerhouse.

Arched windows and door-
ways and newly constructed
skylights bring light into the
interiors of the powerhouse.
To maintain the integrity of
the arched windows, grilles
serve as railings and, when
lowered, provide emergency
access to operable windows.

Power House

Nurses' Annex

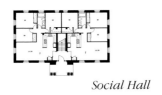

Social Hall

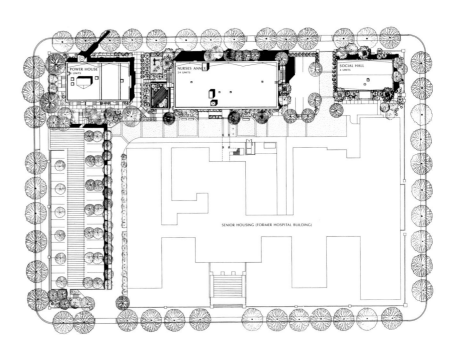

CENTER FOR AIDS SERVICES

OAKLAND, CALIFORNIA

The Center for AIDS Services offers a startlingly ingenious example of the long-established genre of creatively reusing loft space. In a nondescript 6,200-square-foot (558-square-meter) warehouse in Oakland, California, ELS/Elbansi & Logan with Guillermo Rossello created a masterful interior on a very restricted budget that provides a sense of dignity to the center's clients as well as an uplifting, cozy home atmosphere throughout.

The former grocery store, then engineering firm headquarters, appealed to the Center for Aids Services in that all its functions could fit on one level, quite a different setup than the Center faced in its then current home—a Victorian house subdivided into three flats. A non-profit group with limited funding, the Center wanted to move into the warehouse (then set up for the engineering firm) with minimal changes. The building was gutted, leaving one of the existing mezzanines intact.

The space design is simple yet brilliant. Running diagonally the length of the loft is a serpentine wall. This undulating wall provides a barrier between public functions, such as the reception area, living and dining rooms, and child care room, and private functions, such as counseling, mediation and staff offices, therapeutic message rooms, TV lounge, and the food bank. On the public side, the ceiling rises full height, exposing structural and mechanical systems and allowing natural light to enter through existing skylights. On the private side, the ceiling is lower, creating more intimate spaces that nevertheless receive natural light through a two-layered skylight system.

As the executive director said, "What is most wonderful about the design is the curving wall. It almost acts as an arm that reaches out and encircles people."

A gently curving wall effectively separates public and private functions in the Center. On the public side, the wall behind the living room's fireplace encloses the child-care center.

ALL PHOTOS: DAVID WAKELY

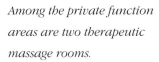

Windows in the serpentine wall were designed to provide security yet privacy, such as the office window overlooking the living room.

The serpentine wall leads from the entrance through the loft to the dining room.

Among the private function areas are two therapeutic massage rooms.

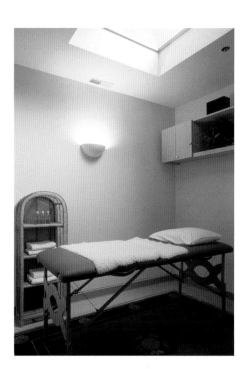

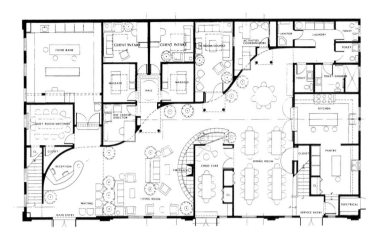

VISITOR CENTER

CHARLESTON, SOUTH CAROLINA

The two restored antebellum railroad structures present strikingly different façades. The brick-enclosed structure houses a visitor's center (below, right), while the open shed shelters the trolley cars.

A popular tourist destination in the Old South is Charleston, where in 1931 citizens helped form the first historic district in the United States. That twenty-block residential area has more than doubled in size and in its carefully preserved state chronicles the city's mid- to late-eighteenth-century architecture. That section of town, however, was obviously not designed to accommodate the vehicular traffic of the late twentieth century. Therefore, to allow easy transport there and back, the city of Charleston developed the new Visitor Reception and Transportation Center. The center itself occupies historic buildings, located nearby in an area containing the largest collection of antebellum railroad structures in the country.

The first phase of the center consists of two adjacent 380-foot-long (114-meter-long) buildings whose reuse was conceived by Cooper, Robertson & Partners with NBBJ-Goff-D'Antonio. The brick building fronting a visitor's parking lot was carefully renovated on its exterior and a skylight added to allow natural light into the interiors. Inside the building is an exhibit of the city and region with information and ticket booths and seating. The second building acts as a bus shed, having undergone greater adaptive changes. Its siding was removed and frame rebuilt, turning it into an open structure with shaded waiting areas. It is also used on special occasions as a farmers' market and as a setting for festival events.

PHOTOS: PAUL WARCHOL

Trolley cars shuttle visitors between the visitor center and other historic districts in Charleston. Taken together, the brick-enclosed and the open-air structures provide a delightful setting for local festivals and other events.

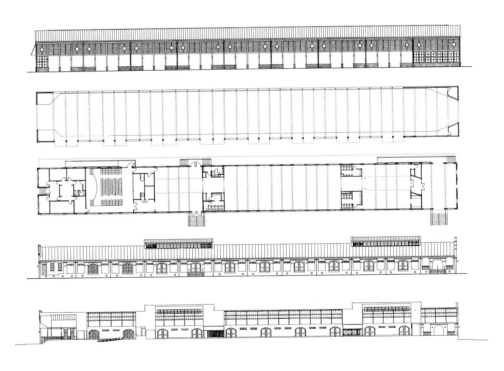

PERE MARQUETTE GALLERY

SAINT LOUIS UNIVERSITY, SAINT LOUIS, MISSOURI

Removal of drywall partitions revealed the beautiful firwood vaulted ceiling. Custom-designed bookshelves reflect the gallery's original use as the university's library. The space is further adorned with new stained glass windows. A tromp l'oeil fresco mural of clouds and sky replaced the tarnished skylight.

When Saint Louis University opened in 1880 as a Jesuit institute of higher learning, DuBourg Hall encompassed the entire university. The showcase of DuBourg Hall was the Pere Marquette library, set in a 10,500-square-foot (945-square-meter) atrium space. Yet, as time passed, the library outgrew this space and the inherent beauty of the Pere Marquette atrium was obscured. Most tragically, its firwood vaulted ceiling was hidden under drywall. Restoration of the space by Mackey Mitchell Associates brought back the original splendor while seamlessly upgrading the building's mechanical and electrical systems.

When the drywall was removed, the architect found the vaulted wood beam ceiling blackened by years of smoke and soot. Restoration specialists in scuba suits were called in to remove asbestos and strip the ceiling with a baking soda solution that restored the wood to its original condition. Wood detailing was meticulously restored. To bring the building in line with current building codes, the mezzanine floors were structurally reinforced and modern heating, cooling, lighting, and fire protection systems introduced. So as not to visually intrude into the old spaces, new mechanical equipment was located on the top level and fed down through pilasters located at the ends of bookcases that were custom designed to reflect the hall's original use. New lighting was cleverly concealed on the tops of the bookcases. Some minor additions included raising the mezzanine handrails and inserting into the windows stained glass depicting symbols of the university or Christianity. A tromp l'oeil fresco mural of clouds in the sky replaced the original skylight.

The spacious main floor of the Pere Marquette Gallery is used for university gatherings and recitals, while the rest displays older volumes from the library. The mezzanine levels showcase the university's growing modern art collection.

DAVID SAUL SMITH UNION

BOWDOIN COLLEGE, BRUNSWICK, MAINE

The creative reuse of a building can make it a much more lively, inviting space. Such was the case with Bowdoin College's David Saul Smith Union. The college wisely envisioned its former field house as a new social center for the campus. With the help of Hardy Holzman Pfeiffer Associates, the once drab, cavernous, clay-floored, undistinguished gymnasium was transformed into a lively, colorful, and light-filled center supporting a variety of student activities.

Designed by Allens and Collens Architects and built in 1913, the field house, known as Hyde Cage, was abandoned in the late 1980s when new campus athletic facilities were constructed. At 40,000 square feet (3,716 square meters), the cage was a huge, open two-story structure capped by a trussed roof and clerestory windows, a space that contained unlimited possibilities for reuse.

For reincarnation of the building, the architects set a ramp along the perimeter of the space to serve as a processional and organizational device; its form echoes that of the former elevated track. This gradually inclining ramp encircles a multistory lounge. Tucked underneath and along the ramp are smaller, enclosed rooms, such as student organization offices, conference rooms, an information center, a bookstore, a 30-seat café, a 150-seat pub, a game room, a copy center, a post office, and other small lounge and social areas located in nooks and crannies.

What makes the David Saul Smith Union a spectacular space is the architect's trademark use of whimsical interior finishes. The ramp's railings undulate and turn. Uniquely shaped pole lights line the ramp much like streetlights—the fixtures are metal fan-shaped shields. Color dominates the interiors, with an enormous, stenciled linoleum rendering of the Bowdoin Sun college seal as the lounge's floor, floral-patterned lounge chairs, and yellow particle board lining some walls.

What makes the David Saul Smith Union successful is that it works. Entering the space is an uplifting experience even on a dreary winter day. Students can study in small spaces off the central lounge, even if a band is performing or a movie is playing in the pub. Not surprisingly, the student union has become one of the most popular buildings on campus.

The multistory lounge is a whimsical ensemble of uniquely shaped pole lights, pink and blue stenciled walls, and undulating ramps.

158

Inserted into the cavernous interior of the former field house, the student union is an exceedingly lively space, with sloping ramps used as a processional and organizational spine. Tucked under and behind the spine are special-use rooms, such as the pub.

THE TROCADERO

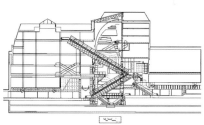

S tep into the Trocadero in London's Piccadilly Circus district and walk into the future. In this 500,000-square-foot (45,000-square-meter) building that occupies an entire block, RTKL Associates, Inc., with Proun Architects, created a glittery, high-tech light and sound show to entertain visitors as they are whisked up through an eight-story atrium to destination SegaWorld.

The Trocadero's design revolves around place making. The driving force was to "control how people move through a particular place and to script what they experience as they advance," according to RTKL's Paul G. Hanegraaf. "The visitor's complete path was mapped out virtually every step of the way, just as a ballet is painstakingly choreographed." The goal was to quickly move people up through the eight-story atrium to SegaWorld but also to encourage enough interest in the lower-level shops and restaurants to prompt a return visit there. The design ultimately places great emphasis not just on the bricks and mortar but also the spaces in between.

The centerpiece of the design is the vertical transportation system, a rocket-shot escalator that moves visitors up through the atrium in 107 seconds. To accommodate the rocket shot, the existing four-story atrium was enlarged to eight stories. To create architecture as entertainment, an elaborate light and sound show was inserted throughout the atrium, with the focal point a gargantuan video wall made of 100-plus 50-inch (127-cm) monitors on a 35-foot (10.7-meter) screen. Live-action video cameras zoom onto visitors caught in moving spotlights.

Architect Hanegraaf stressed that in creating this environment "no stone was left unturned" in the effort to create a consistent, thorough environment. The design does just that.

Inside the historic Trocadero, a fantastic light, sound, and movement show erupts. The main feature is a rocket-shot escalator that carries visitors through the eight-story atrium to SegaWorld at the top of the building.

GARY GROUP

CULVER CITY, CALIFORNIA

Eric Owen Moss has skillfully demonstrated that the extraordinary can be made out of the ordinary. In the first of many adaptive-use schemes in Culver City, Moss turned a deteriorated 1940s steel foundry into a collage of modified catalog parts, symbolic of the area's industrial origins, to create offices for a public relations firm.

The front of the building is located on an alley perpendicular to heavily-traveled Ince Boulevard. So derelict was the long masonry wall facing the main street that the city asked the Gary Group to improve its appearance. The parking lot next to this wall became inspiration to Moss. In essence, he collected the industrial leftovers littering the lot and embedded them in the wall. A grid of windows and planters added a dominant rhythm, and skylights at the building's top created a skyline in this neighborhood of low-rise industrial buildings. A white steel grid straddles the corner to tie side and front together and is visually marked by a fanciful clock tower. The heavily encrusted, long west façade contrasts with the main entrance that recedes behind a new leaning front façade of rust-colored block.

Inside the Gary Group offices, simple building materials—chains draped among concrete block protrusions, rebar ladders, and acrylic panels with assorted metal fasteners—are used as artful decoration. Behind the aesthetics, however, is a series of stories and episodes, according to Moss. It is a tale of how buildings are put together—the obsessive resolution of joints and the glorification of humble support members. New, slightly skewed members, such as the leaning front façade of rust-colored block, heighten the concrete masonry units of the façade and the original structural grid. Important to the overall effect is the insertion of glass and steel into the layers of masonry. And, finally, the catalog of construction components adds a surreal element to the building's dialogue.

The former steel foundry was transformed into a distinctive building designed as a collage of industrial parts, fronted with a leaning false façade.

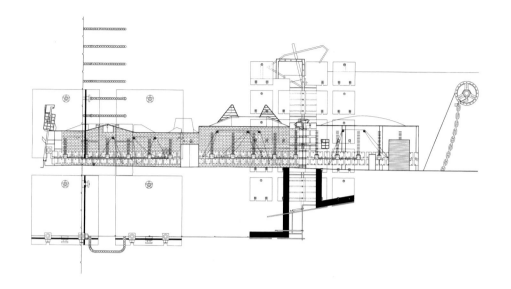

The building's decorated side façade faces a major thoroughfare and announces the industrial motif. A fanciful clock tower acts as a transition from side to front.

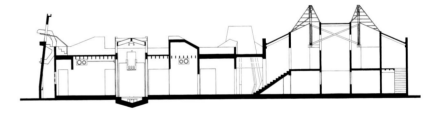

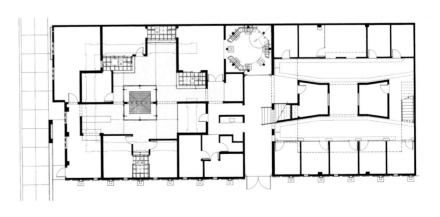

The main entrance is recessed behind a leaning façade of rust-colored block and creates a much differ-ent visual presentation. The white steel-grid clock tower ties the front and side together.

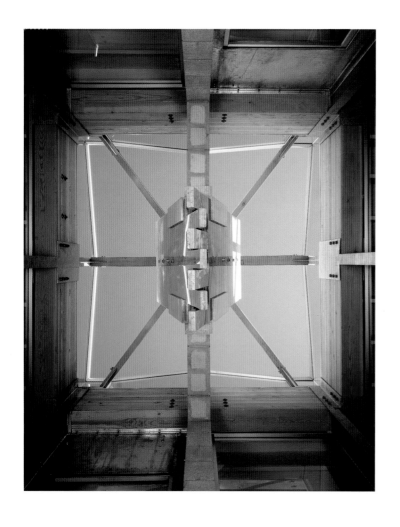

The interior has a unique geometry. The conference room combines an octagon, circle, and square. A sculpture comprised of marble and showerheads crown the small, skylit atrium.

LINGOTTO FACTORY

TURIN, ITALY

Fiat's Lingotto Factory, with its roof test track, will always be considered an icon of industrial modernism. Accordingly, for its transformation into a nonindustrial mixed-use complex, Renzo Piano Building Workshop chose to retain the building's main architectural characteristics while introducing nature as a physical element that unifies it within the urban setting.

Built between 1917 and 1920 and designed by civil engineer Giacomo Matte Trucco, the Turin factory celebrated the automotive production process. In the huge building—five stories, 1,673 feet long (502 meters long), and 80 feet wide (24.4 meters wide), with four inner courtyards—Fiat automobiles were assembled from the ground floor up. As each major step of the assembly took place, each car was moved progressively higher in the building until, when ready for a test run, it was driven out into the test track on the roof.

The Lingotto Factory played a significant role in the lives of Turin residents, for at its peak it employed some 12,000 people. Yet the building became a victim of modern times. In the 1950s Fiat moved much of its operations to other, more modern factories. In the early 1980s new robotic technology made the long assembly lines of Lingotto obsolete. The factory was abandoned but not forgotten; Fiat invited twenty architects to propose new uses and conversion strategies for the former factory.

The architect's proposal envisioned a trade exhibition area, hotel, conference center, concert hall, shops, offices, public space, and underground parking, all housed in a building with much the same appearance as the original. The most significant changes were made to the site. Several ancillary buildings were removed, as were the rail lines that supplied the factory. A landscaped park was established on the west side where the trains once ran; a piazza on the east connects the former factory with the city of Turin. The design brings the garden inside—into the hotel's courtyard and the gardens of the shops, cafés, and restaurants.

In respect for the appearance of the original façade, the architect re-created the stucco that was crumbling on the concrete-frame structure. The large expanses of the curtain wall on the ground floor, where the floor-to-floor height is nearly 25 feet (7.6 meters), were stiffened with the insertion of an aluminum column with circular holes.

While the test track remains, Piano has created a new, more contemporary landmark at Lingotto—the heliport and domed conference suite set on the roof of the building. The conference room for twenty-four persons takes the shape of a bubble and in order to minimize the visible structure, it is built of steel pipes wrapped in double-curved glass panels.

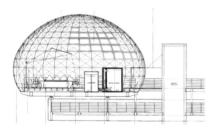

The bubble-shaped conference suite set on the heliport has become a contemporary landmark at Lingotto.

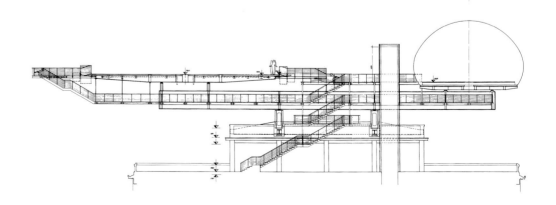

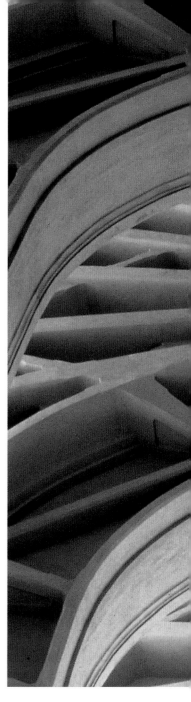

Renovation of Fiat's Lingotto Factory respectfully reinforced the exterior's image while adapting the interior for new uses, including an exhibition hall, concert hall, and hotel. The introduction of greenery, parks, and piazzas was an essential ingredient of the plan.

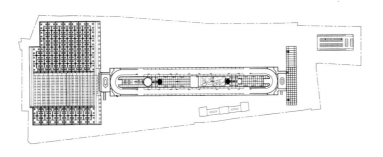

Roof Plan

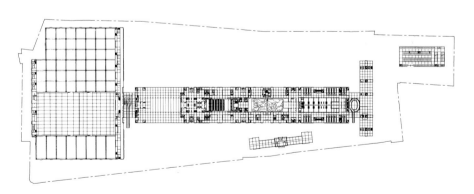

First Floor Plan

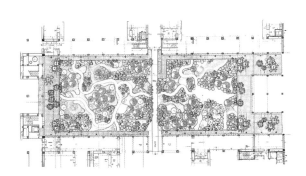

*Aluminum columns bring
visual variety to the ground-
floor hallway and support a
large glass curtain wall.
The hotel surrounds one of
the four courtyards, which
has been landscaped to
resemble a tropical jungle.
Slicing through the center of
the courtyard is a glass-
enclosed corridor.*

LINGOTTO FACTORY **177**

CLARKE QUAY

SINGAPORE

W ith the redevelopment of Clarke Quay, Singapore took its place among major cities with thriving waterfront marketplaces. The execution is different in each city, but for all the concept revolves around the reuse of the warehouses found at old abandoned ports. At Clarke Quay, the original architecture represents an eclectic mix of Singapore warehouse styles dating from 1880 to 1940. The redevelopment of the wharf by ELS/Elbansani & Logan Architects with RSP Architects Planners and Engineers brings together the restoration of these warehouses with the construction of new buildings, all overlaid with a new landscaping plan by EDAW, Inc.

The five-block historic Clarke Quay warehouse district is located at a ninety-degree bend in the Singapore River in close proximity to the downtown high-rise district. The topography nevertheless keeps the district distinct from downtown; the 244,000-feet (22,000-meter) area backs up to the steep hillside of Fort Canning Park, which forms a thick green backdrop. Vacant for several years, the warehouses were in various states of decay. In some, damaged roofs had rotted the floors beneath; trees were growing inside buildings. A decision was made early on to preserve the historic character of the exteriors of these buildings while upgrading the interiors for entertainment, shopping, and dining purposes. The architects relied on replacement of the traditional building materials—plaster, timber window frames, terra-cotta roofing tiles. Contemporary materials were incorporated with restraint. At first glance the new buildings are hard to distinguish, as they were designed to complement their older neighbors in terms of proportion, scale, and detailing.

What makes Clarke Quay work is its pedestrian orientation. All interior streets are closed to vehicular traffic and several plazas were created, including Central Square, which features an open-air shade structure reminiscent of a Victorian bandstand. The street level is devoted to retail and restaurants with entrances and signage visible from the street. Colorful vendors and pushcarts create an intimate, lively, open marketplace. At the eastern edge is the Tropical Garden, a lushly landscaped, quiet riverside park.

On any given day, some 18,000 visitors meander down the pedestrian walkways of historic Clarke Quay, a delightful getaway from nearby modern Singapore.

From across the Singapore River, the revitalized Clarke Quay presents a lively image. Its main street leads from the riverfront of a plaza complete with a Victorian-style gazebo.

PHOTO: TRENDS PUBLISHING INTERNATIONAL LTD.

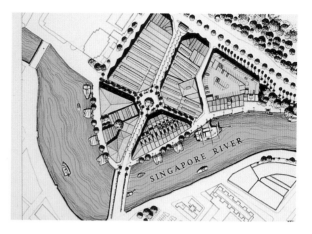

A Teochew-style mansion,
built as a merchant's house
in the nineteenth century,
stands as a riverfront centerpiece. It was painstakingly
restored by sixty craftsmen
from China and now
operates as a banquet
facility. Its style contrasts
with the more restrained
warehouse façades.

PHOTO: DIXI CARRILLO

PHOTO: DIXI CARRILLO

Located in close proximity to the modern high-rises of downtown Singapore, Clarke Quay's low-rise scale welcomes the pedestrian. The waterfront promenade takes on a festive look at night.

PHOTO: TRENDS PUBLISHING INTERNATIONAL LTD.

NAVY PIER

CHICAGO, ILLINOIS

Towers mark the East End Ballroom, the vaulted shape of which is repeated in the new buildings. Navy Pier's Ferris wheel can be seen from great distances. The pier has become a destination for tour and pleasure boats.

As time passes and a city evolves, once special places can be left behind as antiquated relics. Such was the case with Chicago's Navy Pier, which was built to extend over Lake Michigan in 1916. A destination for freight and passenger boats and a public park as well, the pier contained a 2,300-foot-long (690-meter-long) freight shed culminating at the east end in a vaulted ballroom. The pier began its decline in the 1930s; in 1989 the city and state finally agreed on a plan for its revitalization, including a design competition. Selected to redesign Navy Pier, VOA Architects and Benjamin Thompson & Associates, Inc. (now BTA) envisioned the pier as a lively public place rather than a private enclave or a monumental design.

The pier's orientation as a public recreational place is announced by Gateway Park, 19 acres (7.6 hectares) planted with linden, magnolia, crabapple, and honey locust trees at the west end of the pier. Both ends of the pier are punctuated with towers. At the west end, they recall the original ones on site and frame the Head House. At the east, the towers sit on both sides of the ballroom. Between, the building forms intentionally recall the original freight sheds, with one exception: the walls are all glass to allow views into retail shops and restaurants. At the center of the long line of sheds is the Festival Hall (with a solid metal roof) and the Crystal Gardens (with an open glass room). The three arched-vault tensile structures of the Skyline Stage reinforce the ballroom's image.

Navy Pier announces itself with special elements such as the eleven-story-high Ferris wheel and the Skyline Stage. The architects used white materials for the Skyline Stage, the ferris wheel, and the vaulted and sloped roofs in order to catch the sun, as a sailboat's white sails would on Lake Michigan. Historically, Navy Pier was considered the common man's boat, a place to get on Lake Michigan, look back at the fabulous City of Chicago, fish, and enjoy cool lake breezes in the hot summer weather. Fortunately, that special place has been returned to the city.

PHOTO: RICHARD FAWELL

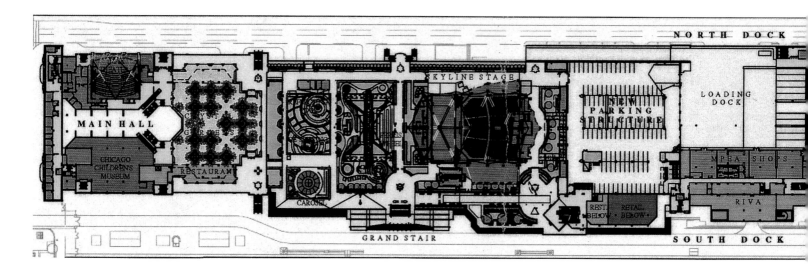

Navy Pier juts out from the Chicago shoreline into Lake Michigan. Fronted by Gateway Park, the whiteness of the pier's buildings is meant to catch the sun as a sailboat's white sails do.

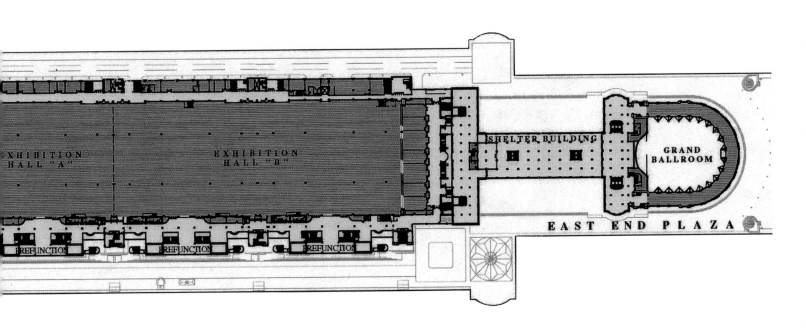

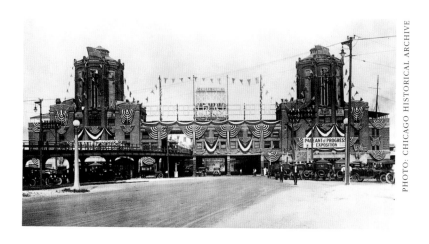

The pier's glass-sided pavilions and other buildings are set between the Head House at the west end and the Ballroom at the east, both marked by their original towers. Originally, the pier housed a number of exhibitions, such as the Pageant of Progress, seen opposite, middle. Its vaulted ballroom was a popular recreational spot.

DIRECTORY and PROJECT CREDITS

RESTORATION, RECONSTRUCTION

New Amsterdam Theater, New York, New York
Hardy Holzman Pfeiffer Associates
902 Broadway, New York, New York 10010
Phone: 212-677-6030
Fax: 212-979-0535
Hugh Hardy, FAIA, *partner-in-charge*; Stewart Jones, *project director*; Maya Shali, *project architect*; John Mueller, *construction architect*; Kristina Walker, *interiors*.

Client: Disney Enterprises, Inc. *Structural engineer*: Desimone Chaplin and Dobryn. *MEP*: Edwards and Zuck. *Theater*: Theater Projects Consultants. *Acoustics*: Jaffee Holden Scarbrough Acoustics. *Lighting*: Fisher Maranzt Renfro Stone. *Historic restoration consultant*: Building Conservation Associates. *Code*: Jerome S. Gillman Consulting Architect. *Construction manager/general contractor*: Tishman Construction.

Fisher Fine Arts Library (Formerly the Furness Building, University Library), University of Pennsylvania, Philadelphia, Pennsylvania
Venturi, Scott Brown and Associates, Inc.
4236 Main Street, Philadelphia, Pennsylvania 19127
Phone: 215-487-0400
Fax: 215-487-2520
Robert Venturi, *principle-in-charge*; David Marohn, *associate-in-charge*; Brett Crawford, *project manager*; Chris Appleford, Denise Scott Brown, David Franke, Rich Mohler, Tom Purdy, Mark Schlenker, Mark Stankard, Nancy Rogo Trainer.

Client: Trustees of the University of Pennsylvania, Department of Facilities Planning and Furness Building Committee. *Historical consultant*: CLIO Group. *Restoration*: Marianna Thomas Architects. *Structural engineer*: Keast & Hood Co. *Mechanical engineer*: Marvin Waxman Consulting Engineer. *Electrical engineer*: Irving Schwartz Associates. *Elevator*: John A. Van Deusen & Associates. *Lighting*: Jules Fisher & Paul Marantz. *Fire protection*: Thomas Goonan Associates. *Security*: Chapman & Ducibella. *Acoustics*: Ostergaard Associates. *Construction costs*: Arena & Co. *Construction Manager*: R.M. Shoemaker Co.

Old Executive Office Building, Washington, D.C.
Einhorn Yaffee Prescott
The Argus Building, Broadway at Beaver, PO Box 617, Albany, New York 12201
Phone: 518-431-3300
Fax: 518-431-3333

Como Park Conservatory, Saint Paul, Minnesota
Symmes Maini & McKee Associates/Windsor Faricy
801 Nicollet Mall, Suite 1600, Minneapolis, Minnesota 55402
Phone: 612-332-3654
Fax: 612-332-3626
Richard Faricy, FAIA, *principal-in-charge*; Donald J. Leier, *project architect*; Bruce A. Tackman, *project manager*. *Engineers*: BKBM Professional Engineers.

Client: City of Saint Paul, William Pesek, *project manager*.

Stanford Memorial Church, Stanford University, Palo Alto, California
Hardy Holzman Pfeiffer Associates
811 West Seventh Street, Suite 430, Los Angeles, California 90017
Phone: 213-624-2775
Fax: 213-895-0923
Norman Pfeiffer, *partner-in-charge*; Stephen Johnson, *associate partner*; Kenneth Drucker, *project manager*; David Senninger, *project architect*.

Client: Stanford University. *Structural engineer*: H. J. Dengenkolb Associates. *Construction manager*: Dinwiddie Construction Company. *Conservator*: Conservation Department, M. H. DeYoung Museum. *Stained glass*: McKernan Satterlee Associates, Inc.; Judson Studios; Association of Restoration Specialists, Inc.; Cummings Studio Stained Glass. *Mosaics*: Tracy Power, Object Conservation; Ralph McIntosh. *Stone*: Richard Pieper, Joel C. Snodgrass. *Decorative painting*: Fine Arts Conservation Lab. *Acoustics*: Paoletti Associates. *Mechanical*: Laws and Associates. *Lighting*: PHA Lighting Design Inc. *Sprinkler*: Rolf Jensen & Associates Inc. *Organ consultant*: John DeCamp; C. B. Fiske Organs. *Specifications*: I. M. Spec/Construction Specifications Consulting. *Building Department*: Santa Clara County. *Electrical*: Hansen & Slaughter.

Joseph Pennock House, Chester County, Pennsylvania
Susan Maxman & Partners, Architects
123 South 22nd Street, Philadelphia, Pennsylvania 19103
Phone: 215-977-8662
Fax: 215-977-9742
Missy Maxwell, Susan Maxman, Thomas Hecht, Robert Hotes.

Architectural consultant: John Dickey. *Client*: Mark and Anna Myers. *Historical documentation*: Alice Kent Schooler, *Architectural Historian*; Professor Bernard Herman, University of Delaware. *Structural analysis*: Richard I. Ortega, P.E. *General contractor and mason*: James Groff. *Prime interior finish and structural carpentry*: Curt Evans. *Roof, windows, and structural carpentry*: James Stoner.

Shakespeare's Globe Theatre, London, England
Pentagram Design Limited
11 Needham Road, London W11 2RP England
Phone: 0171 229-3477
Fax: 0171-727-9932
Theo Crosby, *partner-in-charge*; Jon Greenfield, *project architect*; Ruth Johnson, Bruno Paolucci, Amy Husian, *design team*.

Client: International Shakespeare Globe Center. *Structural/services*: Buro Happold. *Theater*: Michael Holden & Associates. *Quantity surveyors*: Boyden & Co. *Sprinklers*: Gem Consultants. *Historic plastering*: Bruce Induni. *Timber framing contractor*: McCurdy & Co. *Thatching contractor*: Thatching Advisory Service. *Concrete contractor*: CJ O'Shea Ltd. *General building contractor*: Charby Builders, Ltd.

Adelbert Administration Building, Case Western Reserve University, Cleveland, Ohio
R.M. Kliment & Frances Halsband Architects
255 West 26th Street, New York, New York 10001
Phone: 212-243-7400
Fax: 212-633-9769
R.M. Kliment, *partner-in-charge*; Frances Halsband, *collaborating partner*; Richard L. McElhiney, *associate-in-charge*; Christopher R. Borchardt, George D. Hallowell, Michael A. Nieminen, Joseph Singer, Mark H. Wright, *design team*.

Structural engineer: Barber & Hoffman. *Mechanical/electrical engineer*: Byers Engineering. *Specifications*: Robert Schwartz & Associates. *Lighting*: H. M. Brandston & Partners. *Acoustics*: Robert A. Hansen Associates. *Construction manager*: The Krill Company.

Wingspread, Racine, Wisconsin
The Hillier Group Architects
500 Alexander Park CN23, Princeton, New Jersey 08543
Phone: 609-452-8888
Fax: 609-452-8332
Alan Chimacoff, *project principle*; Stephen Diehl, *project architect*; Annabelle Radcliffe-Trenner, *preservation consultant*; Russell Swanson, *project manager*.

Structural engineer: Robert Silman, Robert Silman Associates. *Associated architect*: Vinci-Hamp, Kirsten Kingsley, *project manager*. *Construction managers*: Bentley & Son—Robert Stelter, contractor, Kevin Higgs, project superintendent.

Client: The Johnson Foundation—Charles Bray, *president*; Scott Weas, *manager of construction management for SC Johnson & Son, Inc.*; Louis Berg, *director of administrative services for the Johnson Foundation*.

The Homer Building, Washington, D.C.
Shalom Baranes Associates
3299 K Street NW, Suite 400, Washington, DC 20007
Phone: 202-342-2200
Fax: 202-342-1569
Shalom Baranes, FAIA, *principal-in-charge, lead designer*; Gary Martinez, *project manager*; Patrick Burkhart, *senior designer*; Gerald Tritschler, *project architect*; Kathleen Jones, *construction phase services*.

REHABILITATION

Ellis Island National Museum of Immigration, New York Harbor, New York
Beyer Blinder Belle/Notter Finegold + Alexander, Inc. Associated Architects
41 East 11th Street, New York, New York 10003
Phone: 212-777-7800
Fax: 212-475-7424
John Belle, *partner-in-charge*; Dr. James Marston Fitch, *historic preservation*; James G. Alexander, *principal*. James W. Rhodes, Sherman Morss, Jr., Vincent Benic, Bruce Heyl, *project management*.

Owner: National Park Service/U.S. Department of Interior.

Client: Statue of Liberty/Ellis Island Foundation. *Civil engineer*: Lockwood, Kessler & Bartlett. *Structural engineer*: Robert Silman Associates. *Mechanical and electrical engineer*: Syska & Hennessy. *Lighting*: Jules Fisher & Paul Marantz; *Cost consultant*: Hanscomb Associates. *Management consultant*: Robert Jacobs Associates. *Life safety*: Rolf Jenson & Associates. *Marine engineering*: Sydney M. Johnson & Associates. *Historic landscape architect*: Bruce Kelly. *Landscape architect*: Hanna Olin, Ltd. *Specifications*: Stephen Tucker. *Construction management*: Lehrer McGovern Bovis, Inc.

Fleet Bank, Albany, New York
Einhorn Yaffee Prescott
The Argus Building, Broadway at Beaver, PO Box 617, Albany, New York 12201
Phone: 518-431-3300
Fax: 518-431-3333

Mission Inn, Riverside, California
ELS/Elbansi & Logan Architects
2040 Addison Street, Berkeley, California 94704
Phone: 510-549-2929
Fax: 510-843-3304
Barry Elbansani, *principle-in-charge*; Kurt Schindler, *project architect*; David Fawcett, Steven Heisler, Larry Mack, and Michele Vonk, *project team*.

Client: Chemical Bank, New York. *Historic consultant*: Architectural Resources Group. *Interiors*: A.T. Heinsbergen & Company. *Structural engineer*: Johnson & Neilsen. *Mechanical and electrical engineer*: JCA. *Landscape architect*: EDAW. *Lighting*: Gernald Associates. *General contractor*: HCC Contractors.

Preservation Park District, Oakland, California
Architectural Resources Group
Pier 9, The Embarcadero, San Francisco, California 94111
Phone: 415-421-1680
Fax: 415-421-0127
Stephen J. Farneth, *partner-in-charge*; Bruce D. Judd, *associate partner*; Kate Johnson, *project manager*. *Owner's representative*: Susanne Hirschen, *project manager*; Matt Sherill, *construction manager*.

Landscape architect: Anthony M. Guzzardo & Associates. *Electrical engineer*: Pete O. Lapid & Associates, Inc. *Structural engineer*: Gong, Neishi, Gon, Inc. *Mechanical engineer*: William Mah. *Contractor*: Pearson & Johnson.

Sheraton Palace Hotel, San Francisco, California
Skidmore, Owings & Merrill, LLP
One Front Street, San Francisco, California 94111
Phone: 415-981-1555
Fax: 415-398-3214
Lawrence Doan, *project partner*; John Merrill, *design partner*; Edward McCrary, *project manager*; Stanford Huges, *senior interior designer*; Navin Emin, *senior structural engineer*; Hamed Fatehi, *structural engineer*; Michael Wilson, *senior technical coordinator*.

U.S. District Court of Appeals, San Francisco, California
Skidmore, Owings & Merrill, LLP
One Front Street, San Francisco, California 94111
Phone: 415-981-1555
Fax: 415-398-3214
Carolina Woo, *project partner*; Craig Hartman, *design partner*; Edward McCrary, *project manager*; Sharon Cox, *senior designer*; Carolyn Iu, *interiors department head*; Tamara Dinsmore, *senior interiors design*; Fred Powell, *senior technical coordinator/job captain*; Navin Amin, *structural department head*; Hamed Fatehi, *senior structural engineer*; Anoop Mokha, *structural engineer/base isolation*.

Santa Rosa Railroad Depot, Santa Rosa, California
Glenn David Mathews, AIA
85 Mitchell Boulevard, Suite 1, San Rafael, California 94903
Phone: 415-491-4088
Fax: 415-491-4089
Glenn David Mathews, *project architect*; Laura Culberson, *design associate*.

Structural engineer: MKM Engineers. *Mechanical/electrical engineer*: Murakami Engineers. *Civil/environmental engineer*: Brelje & Race. *Testing engineer*: Klienfelder, Inc.

Dumbarton Oaks, Washington, D.C.
Hartman-Cox Architects
1074 Thomas Jefferson Street NW, Washington, DC 20007
Phone: 202-333-6446
Fax: 202-333-3802

Amstel Inter · Continental Hotel, Amsterdam, The Netherlands
RTKL Associates Inc.
400 East Pratt Street, Baltimore, Maryland 21201
Phone: 301-528-8600
Fax: 301-385-2455
Associate architect: Erik Lopes Cardozo.

Client: Inter·Continental Hotels.

Saint Andrews Old Course Hotel, Saint Andrews, Scotland
RTKL Associates Inc.
400 East Pratt Street, Baltimore, Maryland 21201
Phone: 301-528-8600
Fax: 301-385-2455
Associate architect: The Hurd Rolland Partnership. *Client*: Old Court Ltd. and The Zimmer Group.

Marsh and McLennan Building, Baltimore, Maryland
RTKL Associates Inc.
400 East Pratt Street, Baltimore, Maryland 21202
Phone: 301-528-8600
Fax: 301-385-2455
Edward Haladay, *principle-in-charge*; Steve Eastwood, *project manager*; Fred Hiser, *project architect*.

Historic restoration inventory: Hord, Coplan and Macht. *Cast iron restoration*: Steven T. Baird Architect & Associates. *Owner*: Stone & Associates, Inc. *Engineer*: RTKL Associates Inc. *Landscape Architect*: LDR International. *General contractor*: Lawrence Construction Co., Inc.

Parlin Memorial Library, Everett, Massachusetts
CBT/Childs Bertman Tseckares Inc.
306 Dartmouth Street, Boston, Massachusetts 02116
Phone: 617-262-4354
Fax: 617-236-0378
Richard J. Bertman, FAIA, *principle-in-charge*; Christos Coios, *project architect*; Alfred Wojciechowski, *senior designer*.

Owner: City of Everett, Mass. *Mechanical/electrical engineer*: Shooshanian Engineers. *Structural engineer*: Aberjona Engineering. *Contractor*: Seaman Bratko Corp. *Acoustical*: Cambridge Acoustical Engineers.

Los Angeles Central Library, Los Angeles, California
Hardy Holzman Pfeiffer Associates
902 Broadway, New York, New York 10010
Phone: 212-677-6030
Fax: 212-979-0535
Norman Pfeiffer, *partner-in-charge*; Hugh Hardy, Malcolm Holzman, *collaborative design partners*; Victory H. Gong, *administrative partner*; Stephen Johnson, *senior project manager*; Kala Somvanshi, *project manager*; Candace Renfro, George Buckmann, *project architects*; Robin Kunz, *project interior designer*; Mark DeMarta, Jeff Poorten, *construction administration*.

Associate architect: Kennard Design Group. *Construction managers*: O'Brien-Kreitzberg (library); Maquire Thomas Partners (west lawn). *General contractors*: Tutor-Saliba Corp. (library) Illig Construction (west lawn). *Historic documentation*: Levin and Associates. *Structural engineer*: Brandow and Johnston Associates. *Mechanical/electrical*: Hayakawa Associates. *Civil engineer*: Benito Sinclair and Associates. *Engineers, west lawn*: Cohn & Kanwar, William Yang and Associates. *Acoustics*: McKay, Conant, Brook, Inc. *Graphics and signage*: Bill Brown and Co., Davies Associates. *Lighting*: Fisher Marantz Renfro Stone. *Landscape*: Lawrence Halprin; Befu Morris Scardina; Campbell and Campbell. *Elevator*: Lerch Bates and Associates. *Security automation*: Electron Systems Associates. *Cost estimator*: Wolf and Company. *Geotechnical engineer*: Crandall/Law Associates. *Conservation advisor*: The J. Paul Getty Museum. *Art conservation*: Tatyana Thompson Associates, Rosamond Westmoreland, Scott Haskins. *Restoration cleaning*: A.T. Heinbergen and Co. *Artifact conservation*: Building Conservation Associates, Brian Consadine; Glenn Wharton. *Preservation advisor*: Mellon and Associates. *Code consultant*: Rolf Jensen & Associates. *Testing consultant*: Certified Laboratories. *Artists*: David Bunn (elevator cabs), Therman Statom (atrium chandeliers), Ann Preston (atrium pole lanterns), Ries Niemi (courtyard grilles), Renee Petropoulos (lobby ceiling); Jud Fine, Mineo Mizuno (west lawn fountain).

Ross Commons, Middlebury College, Middlebury, Vermont
Einhorn Yaffee Prescott
The Argus Building, Broadway at Beaver, PO Box 617, Albany, New York 12201
Phone: 518-431-3300
Fax: 518-431-3333

Schlumberger Factory, Montrouge, France
Renzo Piano Building Workshp s.r.l.
Sede Sociale ed Amministrativa, via P.P. Rubens, 29-16158 Genova, Italy
Phone: 39-010-61711
Fax: 39-010-6171350
B. Plattner and N. Okabe, *associates-in-charge*; T. Hartman, S. Ishida, J. Lohse, R. Piano, D. Rat, G. Saintjean, J. F. Schmit, P. Vincent; *with*: M. Alluyn, A. Gillet, F. Laville, G. Petit, C. Susstrunk.

Client: Compteurs Montrough (Schlumberger Ltd.). *Cost control*: GEC. *Engineer, tension structure*: P. Rice. *Landscaping*: A. Chemetoff, M. Massot, C. Pierdet. *Interiors*: M. Dowd, J. Huc.

ADAPTIVE USE

Reception and Training Building, Massachusetts Water Resources Authority, Boston, Massachusetts
Tsoi/Kobus & Associates Architects, Inc.
1 Brattle Square, PO Box 9114, Cambridge, MA 02238
Phone: 617-491-3067
Fax: 617-864-0265
Edward T. M. Tsoi, FAIA, *principle Client*: Massachusetts Water Resources Authority. *General contractor*: The Modern Continental Construction Co., Inc. *Construction manager*: ICF Kaiser Engineers, Inc. *Historical preservation consultant*: McGinley Hart Associates. *Structural engineer*: Weidlinger Associates. *MEP Engineer*: SAR Engineering, Inc.

Tindeco Wharf, Baltimore, Maryland
Cho, Wilks & Benn Architects
200 North Charles Street, Baltimore, Maryland 21201
Phone: 410-576-0440
Fax: 410-332-8455
David Benn, *principal-in-charge Client*: Tindeco Wharf Partnerhsip; *Mechanical/electrical engineer*: Egli & Gompf, Inc. *Structural engineer*: Michael J. Walkley.

Mercy Family Plaza, San Francisco, California
Sandy & Babcock, Architect
PO Box 640777, 1349 Larkin Street, San Francisco, California 94164-0777
Phone: 415-673-8990
Fax: 415-441-3767
James Babcock, *partner-in-charge*; M. Paul Schwartz, *project architect*. *Structural engineer*: Peter Culley & Associates. *Mechanical/civil engineer*: Hawk Engineers. *Landscape consultant*: Anthony M. Guzzardo & Associates. *Historic preservation consultant*: Page & Turnbull, Inc. *Financing*: The John Steward Company. *General contractor*: Midstate Construction Corporation. *Sponsor*: Sisters of Mercy.

Center for AIDS Services, Oakland, California
ELS/Elbansi & Logan Architects with Guillermo Rossello
2040 Addison Street, Berkeley, California 94704
Phone: 510-549-2929
Fax: 510-843-3304
David Petta, *principle-in-charge*; Guillermo Rossello, *project designer*; D. Jamie Rusin, *project architect*.

Interior designer: Institute of Business Designers, Northern California Chapter. *Lighting designer*: Architectural Lighting Design; David Malman. *Major donors*: The James Irvine Foundation, The San Francisco Foundation, The Crescent Porter Hale Foundation, The Clorox Co., David Clayton, Jerome Byrne, Esq.

Visitor Reception and Transportation Center, Charleston, South Carolina
Cooper, Robertson & Partners
311 West 43rd Street, New York, New York 10036
Phone: 212-247-1717
Fax: 212-245-0361
Jacqueline T. Robertson, FAIA, *partner-in-charge*.
Associated architect: BOHM-NBBJ, Inc. *Client*: City of Charleston. *Mechanical/electrical/plumbing and structural*: D.S.A. Group Inc. *Exhibition*: Lyons/Zaremba, Inc. *Surveys/soils*: Soil and Materials Engineers, Inc.

Pere Marquette Gallery, Saint Louis University, Saint Louis, Missouri
Mackey Mitchell Associates
800 Street, Louis Union Station, Suite 200, Saint Louis, Missouri 63105
Phone: 314-421-1815
Fax: 314-421-5206
Eugene J. Mackey III, John Guenther, Sara Koester, Susan Prunchnickl, *project team*.

Client: Saint Louis University. *Lighting consultant*: Lam Partners Inc. *General contractor*: Tarleton Corporation. *Structural engineer*: Alper Ladd. *Mechanical engineer*: Corrigan Co. *Electrical engineer*: Kaiser Electric. *Code compliance*: Code Consultants. *Stained glass windows*: Emil Frei.

David Saul Smith Union, Bowdoin College, Brunswick, Maine
Hardy Holzman Pfieffer Associates
902 Broadway, New York, New York 10010
Phone: 212-677-6030
Fax: 212-979-0535
Malcolm Holzman, *partner-in-charge*; Pamela Loeffelman, *senior associate*. *Associate architect*: Barba Architecture & Preservation. *Structural engineer*: Swift Engineering. *Mechanical/electrical engineer*: Enterprise Engineering, Inc. *Acoustical/audio-visual*: Shen, Milsom & Wilke, Inc. *Landscape*: Mohr & Serdan. *Construction manager*: HP Cummings Construction Co. *Stencil artist*: Toni Wolf. *Owner*: Bowdoin College.

The Trocadero, London, England
RTKL Associates Inc.
400 East Pratt Street, Baltimore, Maryland 21202
Phone: 301-528-8600
Fax: 301-385-2455

Associate architect: Proun Architects. *Client*: Buford Group Plc.

Gary Group, Culver City, California
Eric Owen Moss Architects
8557 Higuera Street
Culver City, California 90232
Phone: 310-839-1199
Fax: 310-839-7922
Eric Owen Moss, *principal-in-charge*; Jay Vanos, *project architect*; Todd Conversano, Scott Nakao, Loren Beswick, Sumathi Ponnambalam, Evelyn Tickle, Lawrence O'Toole and Mathia Johannsen, *design team*.

Structural engineers: Davis/Fejes Design. *Mechanical engineer*: AEC Systems. *Electrical engineer*: California Associated Power. *Lighting*: Saul Goldin. *Plumbing*: MB&A. *Steel furniture*: Tom Farrage. *Construction management*: A. J. Construction *General contractor*: Jamik, Inc.

Lingotto Factory, Turin, Italy
Renzo Piano Building Workshop s.r.l.
Sede Sociale ed Amministrative, via P.P. Rubens, 29-16158 Genova, Italy
Phone: 39-010-61711
Fax: 39-010-6171350
S. Ishida, *associate-in-charge*; P. Ackermann, E. Baglietto; A. Calafati, M. Carroll *test track, landsaping, south tower*; M. Cattaneo, *interiors*; A. Carisetto, G. Cohn, F. Colle, P. Costa, M. Cucinella, *pavilion five*; S. De Leo. A. De Luca, S. Durr, K. Fransen, A. Giovannoni, C. Hays, G. Hernandez, C. Herrin, W. Kestel, P. Maggiora, D. Magnano, M. Mariani. K.A. Naderi, T. O'Sullivan, D. Paino, *completion*; M. Possato Piano, A. Sacchi, S. Scarabicchi, *public floor, hotel, offices*; P. Sanso, A. Stadlmayer, R. V. Truffelli, *completion*; M. Varratta, *fair center, concert hall*; N. Van Oosten, H. Yamaguchi.

Client: Lingotto S.r.l. *Structural and mechanical engineering*: Ove Arup & Partners (concept design), A. I. Engineering, Fiat Engineering (final design); *Acoustics*: Arup Acoustic, Müller Bbm; *Cost control*: Davis Langdon Everest. *Theater*: Techplan. *Exhibition area management*: ECL; *Commercial*: CSST. *Lighting*: P. Castiglioni. *Graphic design*: P. L. Cerri, ECO S.p.A. *Compliance*: F. Santolini. *Site supervision*: Studio Vitone e Associati (fair center), F. Levi, G. Mottino (second phase). *Contractor*: Fiat Engineering, Turin (pavilion five). *Temporary association of contractors*: Recchi, Pizzarotti, Guerrini, Rosso, Borinie Prono.

Clarke Quay, Singapore
ELS/Elbansi & Logan Architects
2040 Addison Street, Berkeley, California 94704
Phone: 510-549-2929
Fax: 510-843-3304
Carol Shen, Alexander Achimore, Al Costa, David Fawcett, Tom Monahan, Cheryl Morgan, Guillermo Rossello.

Local architect and engineer: RSP Architects Planners & Engineers. *Landscape architect*: EDAW, Inc. *Client*: DBS Land/Raffles International Limited. *Economic consultant*: Economics Research Associates (ERA). *Lighting design*: Architectural Lighting Design.

Navy Pier, Chicago, Illinois
BTA/VOA Associates, Joint Venture
BTA Architects Inc. (formerly Benjamin Thompson & Associates, Inc.)
1 Story Street, Cambridge, Massachusetts 02138
Phone: 617-876-4300
Fax: 617-661-9213

VOA Associates Inc.
224 South Michigan Avenue, Suite 1400, Chicago, Illinois 60604
Phone: 312-554-1400
Fax: 312-554-1412
Herb Gallagher, Thomas Green, *partners-in-charge*; James Van Sickle, Richard Fawell, *project architects*; Anthony Ricci, *administration*; Benjamin C. Thompson, Jr., Jane Thompson, *project planners*; Fred Groff, Benjamin Thompson, Denise Henrich Thompson, Diana Tracey, Monte Riggs, Toby Gabranski, Kecia Gifford, Jason Spriner, Joie Watson, Christopher Crowley, *design team*.

Landscape architects: Office of Dan Kiley, Jacobs/Ryan Associates. *Engineering management & civil engineering*: Consoer Townsend Environdyne Engineers, Inc. *Mechanical engineering*: Globetrotters Engineering Corporation. *Electrical engineering*: Environmental Systems Design, Inc. *Structural engineering*: Rubinos & Mesia Engineers, Inc. *Engineering peer review*: Consultants International LTD. *Structural peer review*: Nayyar & Nayyar International,Inc. *Acoustics*: Kirkegaard & Associates, Inc. *Sound AV/acoustics*: Cline Kirkegaard & Associates. *Food service*: Cini-Little International, Inc. *Fire protection*: Rolf Jensen & Associates, Inc. *Theater*: Schuler & Shok, Inc. *Performance tent*: Birdair, Inc.

AUTHORS' NOTES

Nora Richter Greer is a freelance writer living in Washington, D.C., and author of *Architecture as Response: Preserving the Past, Designing for the Future: Einhorn Yaffee Prescott* (Rockport Publishers, 1998). As a communications consultant specializing in architecture and urban affairs, Ms. Greer's work runs the gamut from public relations and marketing to writing and editing newsletters, magazine articles, and books. Previously, she was senior editor at *Architecture Magazine* and editor of the National Trust for Historic Preservation's *Forum* magazine and newsletter. She is the author of two books on housing the homeless, *The Search for Shelter* and *The Creation of Shelter*, published by the American Institute of Architects. A graduate of Connecticut College, Ms. Greer received a master's degree of science in journalism from Northwestern University and is currently completing a master's degree of arts in creative writing at Johns Hopkins University.

Hugh Hardy, FAIA, cofounded Hardy Holzman Pfeiffer Associates, one of the nation's leading planning, architectural, and interior design firms, in 1967. HHPA has created an unusually diverse portfolio of innovative architecture, responding to the needs and imagery of each commission. In recognition of its versatility, the firm has been honored by architectural, civic, and preservation groups with over one hundred design awards. Mr. Hardy has been responsible for important restoration and expansion projects (the New Amsterdam Theater and the Rainbow Room), contextual residential high-rises (Riverbank West and the Siena in Manhattan), and significant urban renewal plans (planning and design for Bryant Park). In continuing service to his profession, Mr. Hardy lectures regularly and is active in numerous professional and civic organizations, such as the National Council on the Arts, a presidential appointment.